CONSENT IN MEDICINE

King Edward's Hospital Fund for London

King Edward's Hospital Fund for London is an independent foundation, established in 1897 and incorporated by Act of Parliament 1907, and is a registered charity. It seeks to encourage good practice and innovation in the management of health care by research, experiment and education, and by direct grants.

Appeals for these purposes continue to increase.

The Treasurer would welcome any new sources of money, in the form of donations, deeds of covenant or legacies, which would enable the Fund to augment its activities.

Requests for the annual report, which includes a financial statement, lists of all grants and other information, should be addressed to the Secretary, King Edward's Hospital Fund for London, 14 Palace Court, London W2 4HT.

CONSENT IN MEDICINE

Convergence and divergence in tradition

Edited by
G R Dunstan and Mary J Seller

King Edward's Hospital Fund for London

Typeset by Rowland Phototypesetting Ltd,
Bury St Edmunds, Suffolk
Printed in England by Hollen Street Press
Bound by Robert Hartnoll Ltd

Distributed for the King's Fund by Oxford University Press

ISBN 0 19 724622 2

King's Fund Publishing Office
126 Albert Street
London NW1 7NF

CONTENTS

Acknowledgement

The Group is indebted to Miss Carolynne Beech, who transcribed the taped record of many of our conversations.

PARTICIPANTS

P A Byrne BA BPhil, Lecturer in the Philosophy of Religion, King's College, London

G R Dunstan MA HonDD FSA, F D Maurice Professor of Moral and Social Theology, and a Director of the Centre of Law, Medicine and Ethics, King's College, London

Sir Immanuel Jakobovits PhD DD, Chief Rabbi of the British Commonwealth

E Stewart Johnson BSc MB BS PhD LRCP MRCS, Reader in Pharmacology, and a Director of the Centre of Law, Medicine and Ethics, King's College, London; Honorary Consultant, City of London Migraine Clinic

Elliot E Philipp MA FRCS FRCOG, Honorary Consultant Obstetrician and Gynaecologist, Royal Northern Hospital and City of London Maternity Hospital; and to HM Prison, Holloway

Paul E Polani FRCP FRCOG DCH FRS, Emeritus Professor of Paediatric Research in the University of London; Director of the Paediatric Research Unit, Guy's Hospital Medical School, London

Mary J Seller BSc PhD DSc, Senior Lecturer in Experimental Biology, Guy's Hospital Medical School, London

Brendan Soane BSc(Eng) PhD ARSM DIC STL, Lecturer in Moral Theology, Allen Hall, London

Professor Koichi Bai, of the Faculty of Law in Tokyo Metropolitan University, attended one meeting of the Group

1

CONVERSATIONS OVERHEARD

G R Dunstan

Not all ideas which surface stay above ground; some soon go under and are forgotten. On 7 March 1977, two men walked from the Royal Society of Medicine in Wimpole Street to the underground car park in Cavendish Square, discussing a symposium on Genetic Screening which they had just attended in the Open Section of the Society. One, the medical scientist, had presented a paper; the other, a moral theologian, had chaired the meeting as President of the Section. The moralist observed that he thought he had noticed ethical assumptions in the Jewish contributions to the symposium rather different from those which he took to be general in such discussions: if he was right, were those differences worth discussing? Professor Paul Polani (for it was he) confirmed that there were differences and that to explore them would be profitable. As a result of this conversation (they had now emerged from the underground car park) they wrote to the Chief Rabbi of the British Commonwealth, whom they knew already to be a distinguished authority on Jewish Medical Ethics, and invited his participation in the task. (Unknown to them such an inter-faith and inter-disciplinary discussion had already been mooted between the Archbishop of Canterbury, the Cardinal Archbishop of Westminster and the Chief Rabbi.) With his ready assent, therefore, a group was formed: the Chief Rabbi himself and a Jewish doctor; a Roman Catholic moralist and a Roman Catholic doctor; Professor Polani and a colleague in medical research; the author of this chapter, himself a moralist in the Anglican tradition; and two colleagues at King's College London, the one a clinical pharmacologist, the other a moral philosopher. Unfortunately pressure of other commitments prevented the Roman Catholic doctor from attending any but two early meetings of the Group; the other members have managed to take part in almost every discussion. After the first two exploratory meetings, at which the Chief Rabbi was host, the Group met at King's College about three times a year. Papers were prepared, discussed, revised, and discussed again. A selection of these form the material for this book.

The stated aim was 'to study and discuss selected topics in medical science and practice in the light of the Hippocratic, Jewish and Christian traditions'.

Ethics has to do with mutual expectations: professional ethics with what members of a profession and those whom they serve may properly expect of one another in their professional relationship. We began, therefore, with two trial papers: the first by Mr Peter Byrne, on What may a patient properly expect of his doctor? (Chapter 2); the second, by Dr Stewart Johnson, on Considerations governing a doctor's advice to a patient, subsequently taken into Chapter 7. It emerged from the discussion of both papers that whereas there is today no lack of voices telling doctors their duties, there was as great a need to educate the public in theirs, in what are proper expectations and what improper. Some false expectations rest on an unrealistic belief that all things are possible in modern medicine if only practitioners would try hard enough: on a lack of awareness of random, of sheer chance in individual reactions to routine procedures or medicines, and so of inevitable risk; of the sheer novelty, on the long view, of modern therapeutics and so of the necessarily experimental nature of advancing medical practice. When unrealistic expectations are unfulfilled, disappointment follows; then a sense of grievance, of a right denied; and then, given opportunity and encouragement, the demand for redress, a readiness to sue. Insofar, furthermore, as a certificate of ill-health or of disability is a passport to certain financial or social benefits, the doctor as certifier can be brought under pressure as a dispenser of tickets and signatures to validate a patient's own assessment of himself; and to be scrupulous or not very obliging in this role is to invite hostility. And pressure of time, with a crowded waiting room, may drive him to give short shrift if not to take short cuts.

Such hostility is not good for medicine. The doctor himself can lessen it, but at cost. His understanding of human nature – what is called now patient psychology – will teach him about the projection of uncertainty, anxiety and anger which cannot inwardly be borne; and his professional training, preparation for his role, will have taught him that he must take some of this upon and into himself if he is not to match thrust with thrust – *vim vi repellere* – and so put the patient further beyond aid. His professional role is, above all, *curare*, to care; and only in caring can he hope sometimes to cure (*sanare*). He cannot expect reciprocity of care. Yet he is entitled to look for a reciprocity in commitment, a willingness in the patient to play a full and honest part, first in disclosing the history and symptoms necessary for the formulation of a diagnosis, and then in the course of therapy prescribed. An extension of the concept of 'medical ethics' to embrace this task of educating potential patients in expectation, commitment and cooperation is, therefore, a necessary balance, and one which may yet keep doctors and patients from falling further apart.

But what lies behind or beneath the expectations? Some have, of course, simply a pragmatic justification: experience shows that when taken for granted they benefit the parties. A simple analogy would be the relation of car-drivers to the policeman directing traffic at a busy intersection: their relationship to him, and their conduct towards one another, are governed by their recognition and acceptance of conventional signals – stance, posture, gesture of hand and arm. The analogy has power when seen in a highly stylised performance in the Piazza Venezia, say, or in some other animated junction of routes in a European city. It is not altogether devoid of power when the signals are reduced to a sequence of lights, red, amber and green, electronically controlled; for the lights are invested with the authority of law, creating an expectation that drivers will relate to one another in conformity with them. But the analogy is too simple, as is the merely pragmatic justification, for the subtlety and variety of mutual expectations in medical ethics. Why *should* a patient act on a doctor's advice – *if* he should? How far *should* a doctor expect a patient to act on his advice, and why? What liberty has a patient to reject his doctor's advice? What liberty has a doctor to decline to meet his patient's wishes? These are the questions which, in discussion, brought us to the assumptions which lie beneath or behind the expectations. They are moral assumptions, first of all; and their morality is grounded, in turn, in certain beliefs about man, religiously or philosophically derived. And at this point the differences in the ethical traditions, Hippocratic, Jewish and Christian, begin to appear.

The knowledge and skill on which the doctor rests his profession – those which he *professes* in his offer of help to patients – are those of medical science; that is, of human biology, anatomy, physiology and pathology clinically applied. In these he is expert. What authority, then, do they give him over his patients? They invest him, first, with the authority inherent in knowledge, and therefore with power. Do they invest him also with moral authority, with authority over persons, that is, of a sort which in conscience they should accept and obey? Here considerations begin to divide. It is inherent in our concept of a profession that the knowledge and skill proper to that profession are exercised under moral control; the control, that is, of the body corporate exercised in the conscientious judgments of practitioners personally. The alternative is unthinkable. No professional man, even in the non-personal, non-caring professions like civil or mechanical engineering, could consent, at the behest of a client, to execute a design which he knew to be in violation of his scientific axioms or of his duty to a wider society. The doctor, in short, has a professional conscience which patients should not expect him to violate. But the other side of the question remains: does the profession of a doctor bind his patients in conscience also? Granted that his medical knowledge can tell him what is good for his patient, what is in his patient's medical interest, has that knowledge in itself such binding authority that the patient is bound to accept the regimen prescribed upon it? To this question the Jewish tradition appeared to answer Yes, the Catholic Christian* tradition to answer No. The Hippocratic tradition yielded no ready answer; one had to be looked for.

Discussion, then, of the two preliminary papers, on what doctor and patient may properly expect of one another, had brought us to this point, that behind the expectations lay, on the one side, moral assumptions inherent in the notion of a profession, and, on the other, moral assumptions about patients which, because they differed from one another, left patients with different degrees of obligation to act upon medical advice. This led us to request further papers on the place of *consent* in medical practice, that is, on the degree of liberty which ought to be allowed to a patient to give or withhold consent in relation to the doctor's obligation to serve that patient's interest in health while living, and in dying well when the time comes to die. The Chief Rabbi wrote on the Jewish tradition (Chapter 3); Father Brendan Soane wrote on the Catholic tradition (Chapter 4).

There is a danger in all such discussions that related issues may become unduly polarised; and this danger is more acute in summary than in fuller exposition. For the refinements in the respective positions the reader is referred to the chapters themselves. 'Doctor's orders' is a phrase which, whatever its status in fiction and casual speech, is one which today's liberal practitioner studiously avoids and actively disowns. He gives advice, he will say, and no more. But 'doctor's orders' are precisely what, in the Rabbinic tradition, the doctor should give and the patient should expect and obey. The doctor's knowledge and professional role invest him with authority. To him is entrusted the duty of serving the patient's interest in life. The patient is under strict duty to enhance that life and to preserve it. It is for the doctor to prescribe the means, and for the patient to accept them.

* The word 'Catholic' is used in this book to denote the moral tradition of Western Christianity developed out of Aristotle in the Middle Ages, and inherited today, not by Roman Catholics only, but by other Christian confessions, as well, notably the Anglican. When we have meant 'Roman Catholic' we have said so.

Since every human life is infinitely precious, every minute of it is precious; it is therefore to be preserved as long as is medically possible, though such treatment is not calculated merely to prolong the dying agony by artificial means. There is no room here for the philosopher's neat distinction between a categorical imperative, 'Accept such and such treatment', and a hypothetical imperative, 'If you want to get better, you must accept such and such treatment', for the patient is already under obligation to want to get better, and to accept the necessary means.

There are, of course, accepted limitations to this theory. A wise doctor would in practice advise and not order, and so advise as to make a willing acceptance more probable. No doctor is infallible. If a patient has serious reason to doubt the wisdom of the advice given him, or of the course prescribed, he may seek another opinion. The doctor is a specialist in medicine, not in morals. When, therefore, there is doubt, not so much about the medical advice as about the implications for life, the patient may properly consult his rabbi for guidance from the religious tradition. The duty to preserve life as long as possible does not entail a duty to prolong suffering. Pain should be relieved by all proper means; and for so long as a doctor feels bound to assist in the preservation of life, so also he is bound to relieve the distress of it to the utmost of his ability. But he may not desist from that task until the death-process has recognisably begun: if an infection like pneumonia should supervene upon an irremediable condition which was not of itself fatal, he is under obligation to treat the infection with a remedy specific to it. Only the onset of the process of dying relieves him of that task. He must assuage the pains, if any, of death; he may not cause death nor hasten it.

On this last duty the Christian tradition is at one with the Rabbinic: the doctor as a servant of life, as an assistant friend in dying, may not kill. Yet the Christian tradition differs from the Rabbinic in the extent of its command over the patient's obedience to medical advice. It accepts the common duty to preserve mind and body in health, and to accept medical help in so doing. Doctor and patient have mutual obligations in this respect, directed to the same end, the patient's good. But in the Christian tradition this good is not so closely identified with the preservation of life, regardless of other considerations, as it is in the Rabbinic tradition. The Catholic tradition within Christianity employs a distinction – albeit a fluid one – between ordinary and extraordinary means of preserving life. These are discussed more fully in Fr Soane's paper. Ordinary means the doctor is under obligation to offer and the patient to accept. Extraordinary means are elective: the patient may decline them if he judges the burden which they impose – physical, emotional, financial, social – more than he is prepared or willing to bear for the sake of prolonging his days. This mitigating concept of undue hardship might extend beyond clinical treatment to way of life: given the choice of a longer expectation of life in a healthier climate, isolated from all that has been familiar, congenial and fulfilling at home, the patient may prefer the shorter if happier life, and decline medical advice to move away. What is physically possible may be, for him, morally impossible; it is beyond the call of duty; he may refuse, without moral censure, an act or a degree of suffering which, in other circumstances, might be held meritorious, morally praiseworthy. The refusal or omission of a course deemed to be life-preserving is, in such a case, not the equivalent of an act of self-destruction.

This judgment is of special importance for a patient, already chronically ill with an irremediable and distressing condition, likely to result in death in a not distant future, who then contracts an acute illness, like pneumonia, for which specific remedies are available. In the Catholic Christian tradition it is a matter of discretion whether a remedy for the pneumonia be administered or not. The decision may be a joint one, if the patient is conscious and competent to decide; or, if not, it would be for the doctor alone, as a clinical decision made in what he judges to be the best interest of his patient. If death followed, the doctor would not be morally culpable by negligence or omission for the death. Here the distinction between perfect and imperfect duties is invoked. As one of our number put it, 'Everyone is under perfect duty not to murder. That is a duty which admits of no exceptions. Whereas the duty to preserve life is an imperfect duty: that is, it does admit of exceptions; it does not tell one to preserve life on each and every occasion. One needs judgment to decide when life is to be preserved and when not . . . And moral impossibilities are one of these things which one must consider in thinking about the imperfect duty to preserve life.'

The inverse case concerns the patient terminally ill and in severe distress. It is the doctor's duty to alleviate that distress, and he has means with which to do it. It may be that the analgesic which he gives, while succeeding in that for which it was intended, in relieving the pain, has a secondary effect of exposing the patient to an attack of pneumonia from which he dies. The death, though foreseeable as a possibility – it is by no means a certainty or even a probability – would then be a secondary and unintended effect of a remedy properly administered; the doctor would not be guilty of that death, even though life was shortened as a consequence of his action. This case illustrates the principle of double effect, which is employed with other applications in Catholic moral theology. The Jewish tradition, too, countenances the relief of suffering in terminally ill patients with medicines which may possibly shorten life, provided that they are not intended to induce death but simply to relieve pain, even if this may unintentionally have fatal consequences.

There has emerged, then, in our discussion, both a fundamental difference between the Rabbinic and the Christian traditions and a practical similarity. When we asked to which side the generality of medical practice inclined, we saw at once that it was towards the Christian (though without attribution) rather than the Rabbinic. Indeed, the doctor's recognition of a patient's liberty to choose was by no means restricted to the more severe or invasive procedures which might fall within the range of 'extraordinary' means. 'Advice' given in the context of, for instance, genetic counselling or the advisability of therapeutic or preventive abortion, may be no more than the objective giving of information, the clarification of options;

though to be well done it would be so done as to enlarge freedom from anxiety, doubt or fear, and so enable the patient to decide. The modern doctor, practising anywhere in Western Europe or North America today – and increasingly so elsewhere, even in such authoritarian countries as Japan – has to work with the principle of 'consent'. In strict law he could be guilty of assault if he did not secure the patient's consent even to touch him, whether for examination or for such a simple procedure as feeling the pulse. For treatment, whether by surgery or by pharmaceutical means, the consent has to be 'informed' consent: the patient is supposed to be made sufficiently aware of its nature, and of its potential benefits and risks, for his consent to be given with understanding. In practice, if the truth be told, consent is more generally given on the basis of trust than of understanding – and trust is essential to a good doctor-patient relationship. But trust is no way of escape from consent. It embodies the reliance of the patient on the doctor's judgment that *if* the nature of the procedure and the balance of benefit and risk were fully understood, the patient would have, and properly, consented to it. On this basis stands the acceptance of proxy consent, for children or patients incompetent to consent for themselves, and the presumed consent on which a doctor acts in emergency. We were so driven, by the course of our argument, to examine the nature of consent, and the philosophy or belief about the nature of man on which it rests. Mr Byrne's paper examines this (Chapter 5).

Granted that this is the modern view, how old is it? Granted that it is now held to be axiomatic in 'secular' medicine, that is in common practice, irrespective of either the Rabbinic or the Christian tradition, does it derive from that Greek tradition which we call Hippocratic? We all assumed that it did, until Professor Polani set out to look for it. It appears from his historical survey (Chapter 6) that this is by no means true. Indeed, the Hippocratic doctor stood much nearer the Rabbinic doctor in that he required his patient to obey whatever course the physician prescribed for him; his was an authoritarian tradition, not a liberal one.

Consent has come into modern practice from another source and by another route. Lacking a lawyer in the Group, we invited Mr Ian Kennedy, a Director of the King's College Centre of Law, Medicine and Ethics, to tell us when the concept came into the purview of the law; and his note, in answer to our question, is appended to Professor Polani's survey. While one root of it lies deep in the common law tradition, in the tort or wrong of assault, its status as a ground for effective action in the courts is a modern one: a creature virtually of this century. Thomas Percival, in his classic treatise *Medical Ethics*[2], does not mention it.

The three traditions with which we began, then, the Jewish, the Christian and the Hippocratic, were examined, not as interesting historical or sociological phenomena, but in relation to practice, as they influence the relationship between doctor and patient. Mr Byrne, in Chapter 5, traces points of difference and similarity between the two religious traditions. But he does this, not from a pose of neutrality – that would be a pose indeed, if it implied that he brought to the examination no assumptions of his own – but as a moral philosopher committed to a tradition which recognises autonomy in human beings, and seeks to protect it up to the point where it begins to encroach upon the autonomy of others or to imperil the common good. The provocation of this philosophical tradition was valuable in our discussion when it drove us back to examine what beliefs lay behind the moral prescriptions of the two religious traditions. *Why*, in the Rabbinic tradition, is every moment of man's life infinitely precious, and so to be cherished to the last, even against the patient's wish to die? *Why* does the classical Christian tradition entrust the patient with a liberty to accept or reject treatment which, if successful, would save his life, but without which he would die; and why does it oblige the doctor to respect that liberty?

These questions are often discussed in terms which become eroded with use, with over-use, sometimes with careless use. Such terms are 'the value' of human life, or 'the worth' of human life. Their use is confused. We may properly ask, of value to whom or of worth by what measurement?

Step by step, false or irrelevant evaluations are excluded when the terms are considered in relation to what care is owed to a patient, the more readily when memory is still tender from the barbarities inflicted by the Nazis on the Jews, and when the mind is aware of Soviet and other maltreatment of dissidents today. The value of a patient's life is not to be measured by its utility, nor his worth even by moral esteem: the socially useless, the morally worthless have yet a value and a worth simply by virtue of their being human. Physically or mentally impaired they may be, yet we recognise in them our common humanity and so impute to them an inherent worth – as coins derive their worth from the imprint of the sovereign's head, however bent, worn or tarnished they may be. There may also be infinite worth in the contribution to the ennoblement of society made by a helpless patient, in whatever state of debility, through the virtues of care and compassion cultivated in those charged tenderly to protect such a stricken life.

In both the Jewish and the Christian tradition this conviction stems from faith in God, in the same God, though differently perceived. It is the common faith that life is the gift of God; that man is made in the image of God, in the image of His eternity, His righteousness, His creative, redemptive and forgiving love. Man's true life is in a covenant of His making in which He has both shown or revealed himself and shown man how he ought to live. Man is called to faithfulness in this covenant. The Jewish tradition, unswerving in its holistic view of man – its belief in the essential unity of his personality – lays its emphasis on the physical nature of man. It is his life – all of it, body, mind, sentience, affections, will – which is infinitely precious to God; through his life, throughout his limited span of time, he is related, bound, to the eternal God and so to the eternity of God. That is why it is his duty to enhance and preserve his life, and the duty of his doctor to assist him in it. Not to do so is a sin, and the doctor must not be a partaker in his sin. Martyrdom, the willing surrender of bodily life, is licit, but only on the severest conditions, only at the extreme demand of faithfulness to the covenant. It would be wrong to risk or sacrifice one life, whether voluntarily or not, for the putative benefit of ten: each life is, in itself, uniquely precious to God.

Christian theology, though it derived from the Jewish consciousness of man and God, came, early in its independent life, under the influence of the Greek philosophies prevalent in its contemporary world. Throughout its history, therefore, it has halted between a holistic and a dualistic interpretation of man: it has confused itself perennially with the concept of the soul. It is an historical fact that this confusion has led, in certain ages, to a devaluing of the body and its passions, to an exaltation of martyrdom, to a scale of values in which 'the flesh', however interpreted, ranked low. It is of the utmost importance that this fact be not allowed to intrude upon the present discussion of the worth of man, or, in particular, into the question why the Christian may licitly consent to or refuse the medical prolongation of his life. The Christian does not welcome death in order that his 'soul' may escape from the prisonhouse of the body and fly to God. Man is one person; the worth of that person is intrinsic; not lessened, not to be denied the protection which is its due, on account of any extrinsic 'worthlessness' or lessening of value by social inadequacy or delinquency or physical or mental handicap. Physical life is an episode in that eternal relation of the person with the God who imprinted its worth upon it. Death, as the natural outcome of physical life, is to be accepted; yet death seen as this mortality in nature is the last enemy, and one that shall be destroyed. The liberty to choose death (though not, normally, to cause it) when prolongation of physical life is an option, stands upon another interpretation of man's being made in the image of God. Man is most like his Creator in his capacity, by the use of the divine gift of reason, to make moral judgments and to follow them. He is not only to do good, or the right, but to choose to do so; and in order to choose he must be free.

It is this doctrine of the freedom of man – expressed variedly in the Christian tradition, by St Paul, say, in one way, by St Thomas Aquinas or Martin Luther in others –

which brings that tradition nearest to the moral tradition in which Socrates is reverenced for the manner of his death. Cherished and revered as the life of the body is – the instrument of all our perceptions and social joys – even that must be renounced if moral betrayal is the price of its survival. The Japanese tradition also is strong on this. That, however, is at the extreme of consideration, far removed from that medical practice which is our theme. (Doctors do not spend most of their time in saving or not saving lives, but in palliating ills.) Yet it is this same ultimate respect for freedom and human autonomy which underlies the doctrine of consent. Again, we caution against extremes. It is one of the fads of the day, in some parts of the West at least, to exalt informed consent into a fetish, to the hindrance of good medicine and to the benefit of none but the litigious.[3] Normal medical practice is conducted on the basis of trust and of the conventions created by and proper to trust. Nevertheless, the Christian moralist and the moral philosopher both assert conviction, theological and philosophical axioms, as the ground for a certain rule of practice: that the best doctor-patient relationship is one in which the patient is so informed about himself, within his capacity for understanding, that he can consent to what is proposed for him or decline; and that his autonomy be respected. He may consent for his own good. He may consent for the good of others, as when he is invited to act as an experimental subject for the acquisition of knowledge not directly intended for his benefit. Without his consent, such experiments or investigations may not be performed. He may refuse consent to proposals of either sort, if that is his settled will. This autonomy is not absolute. It is modified by the condition that it must be exercised reasonably, within a common order of moral values. And it is properly restrained when it threatens the common good: a patient may not refuse notification or even isolation, for instance, if he contracts a particularly threatening infectious disease. But within those limits, and within a moral agent's own scheme of values, it is licit to decide that ill-health, or a shortened life, is preferable to a proposed treatment or modification of life.

We were aware that, in saying this, we closed no questions but rather opened them. Chapter 7, by Dr Johnson and Mr Philipp, carries some of them further. It is the proper task of casuistry to respond to the questions raised in the application of principles to particular cases; this is the function of the *responsa* in the Rabbinic tradition and of interpretation and direction in the Christian. Consent by proxy on behalf of patients who cannot consent for themselves raises questions which cannot always be settled by rule of thumb or in the generalities proper to the Helsinki Code or other such declarations; they are not even readily soluble by law. The law may set one age as that of legal majority; another for marriage or consent to sexual intercourse; but on what criterion can it rely to determine the age at which an adolescent may consent to a surgical operation or to give blood for transfusion, or even an organ for grafting into a twin? May a parent properly consent to the extraction of bone marrow from a child for transfusion into another? Or what is the duty of a doctor whose child-patient may be in peril unless given the blood transfusion to which his parent, a Jehovah's Witness, will not consent? These are cases which trouble the practitioner; the moralist may help him to resolve them, in discussion; he cannot resolve them for him, for he has not the responsibility of practice; he is not *authorised* to decide. The distinction, too, between therapeutic and non-therapeutic experiment – the one designed to find a remedy potentially beneficial to the patient in clinical care, the other designed as research for the advancement of medical knowledge, but without an intended benefit to the subject of investigation – necessary as it is in the formulation of the principles of consent, soon loses its simplicity in the rapid development of modern therapeutics. Insofar as the doctor, even in clinical practice, is a medical scientist, and every patient a unique biological organism whose response even to well-tried remedies may differ from any other, clinical treatment is itself experimental. There are, therefore, those who, in serious discussion of the ethics of practice, abandon the distinction and construct their protective ethics on other grounds.[1] We could, in our conversations, but allude to such questions, not pursue them.

Neither could we explore all the terms, legal and conventional, in which the doctor-patient relationship is formulated. We expressed general dissatisfaction with the language of contract, doubting its aptitude even in a practice where the formal consideration is the direct payment of a professional fee. We found the term 'Covenant' more ample; it can express much when considered in the light of theological tradition, or even in such usage as The Covenant of the League of Nations; but it is bewildering to minds accustomed to deeds of covenant in income tax law, or to restrictive covenants in the transfer of property or land. Yet the questions remain. On what do we ground the obligation commonly accepted by doctors (though now under strain in litigious societies) to give immediate help in a road accident or other emergency? The doctor is under contract to no-one; he can expect no potential beneficiary contract as in the conditions of salvage at sea. But he is covenanted somehow to the injured by his profession of a skill apt to their hurt. He does what he can. The formalities can wait until the patient is under regular care. The Rabbinic tradition would seem to oblige him further. If his clinical training and experience led him to recognise in a fellow man – not his patient, not, so far as he knows, anyone's patient – a condition which he knew to be threatening, it would be his duty to warn that person in some suitable way, if only to get him to seek advice – his duty simply as a physician to a fellow man, every moment of whose life is infinitely precious. This duty to save life and limb, imposed upon anyone able to do so, is based upon the biblical command, 'Thou shalt not stand on thy neighbour's blood'. There is no room for contract here; there is a place for covenanted concern. To exclude contract does not diminish care. All doctors, on all occasions, including voluntary help in emergency, have a duty of care; the law has its own formulae by which to determine when defective care amounts to professional negligence.

Religion and philosophy, we have seen, are fundamental insofar as they underlie our concepts of duty and liberty in practice. They may be important also to the practitioner. If, indeed, he professes a creed with any seriousness, he is bound in some sense to its moral prescriptions. What, then, of patients who profess another creed, or none at all? What of practice in a pluriform or secular society which has modelled its public health services on no such profession? This question is faced in a variety of ways. In the three traditions which we have considered there is common recognition of an obligation to accept into care any patient, regardless of religious persuasion – not unconditionally, but presumptively until a conflict of conviction makes the continuance of the relationship untenable. In statutes like the English Abortion Act 1967, which give qualified permission for medical interventions of which some doctors and nurses disapprove in conscience, clauses are inserted granting them qualified exemption from practice: they may decline to participate in such an operation, except when the necessity for it supervenes upon another operation in which they are engaged and when withdrawal would jeopardise the patient's interest. Regulations which empower doctors to provide means of contraception to the married and unmarried alike recognise the liberty of practitioners to decline in conscience to do so: they may refer patients to another doctor who does not feel so bound. Such formal accommodations to conscience are possible in a tolerant society. Informally each doctor is the monitor of his own conscientious duty. 'A doctor can have no other religion, as a doctor, than that of his patient', it was said more than once in our conversations; though the limitation of the epigram was recognised, and was not received by all of us unreservedly. The doctor has a moral reserve of his own: he knows that there are things which he will not do. But in that broad spectrum of *adiaphora*, matters either morally indifferent or on which diverse moral options are allowable in one society, he feels himself bound by his patient's scruple, either to prescribe what his patient, not his own conscience, will accept, or to refrain from pressing what he would prefer but his patient could not accept. St Paul, in guiding his Corinthian converts on their conduct at dinner, when their host's meat, because bought in the shambles, had been offered sacrificially in slaughter to some pagan divinity, followed a not dissimilar rule.

We undertook our enquiry, five years ago, out of academic curiosity: we saw a question and we sought an answer. We have pursued that enquiry together to our mutual enrichment. We publish some of our working papers now, linked together by this introductory commentary, in the belief that we have explored issues of general importance, and that their wider discussion may help doctors and patients to clarify what they expect of one another in their professional relationship. Our aim is to promote trust, based on respect for professional obligation and personal integrity. Left to themselves, the public media of communication, especially the visual media, excite discussions of medical ethics in terms of either spectacular 'high-technology' medicine or of sensational departures, or threatened departures, from what are assumed to be sacrosanct norms. The threshold, too, between ethical issues and socio-political issues, not itself clearly defined, is easily crossed. There is some gain in public debate so conducted – and it cannot be restricted, anyway, in a liberal society except by responsible self-restraint. But it incurs some loss also, particularly in the engendering of mistrust and fear. There is still room for men of strong convictions, differing convictions, calmly and in amity to exchange ideas.

References

1 Janofsky, Jeffrey and Starfield, Barbara. Assessment of risk in research on children. *Journal of Pediatrics*, vol 98, no 5. May, 1981. pp 842–846.

2 Percival, T. (1803) *Medical Ethics. Or, a Guide to Institutions and Precepts Adapted to the Professional Conduct of Physicians and Surgeons.* Manchester: printed by S. Russell, for J. Johnson, St. Paul's Churchyard, and R. Bickerstaff, the Strand, London.

3 Siegler, M and Goldblatt, A D. Clinical intuition: a procedure for balancing the rights of patients and the responsibilities of physicians. In: Spicker, S F and others. eds. *The law-medicine relation: a philosophical exploration.* Dordrecht, Holland, D Reidel, 1981.

2

WHAT MAY A PATIENT PROPERLY EXPECT OF HIS DOCTOR?

Peter Byrne

I take as my basic assumption that a successful relationship between patient and doctor is conditional on the patient's expectations more or less matching what the doctor has to offer.[1] Thus it is vitally important that the patient go to his doctor with a just and reasonable expectation of what he can provide.

It is easy enough to state in very general terms what expectations the reasonable patient will have of his doctor. He will expect his doctor to help him in preserving or regaining his health. General though this may be, it is enough to rule out many of the motives which patients have in visiting their doctor. Many patients visit a doctor because they wish to gain some social advantage; for example, they would like to have some time off work and regard a sick note as the best way to get it. More excusably, they may go to a doctor ostensibly to seek medical advice when in reality they have a spiritual or emotional problem which medical science cannot treat.

So the reasonable patient will go to his doctor expecting the doctor to use his skills in assisting him to preserve or recover his health. It is important that the expectation be formulated in this way: it will not do to say simply that the patient expects the doctor to give him health. For, of course, there are and always will be limits to what any doctor can achieve. Some conditions have no effective treatments and few treatments can be guaranteed 100 per cent success. It is as well even in an age of remarkable treatments and cures to have a just sense of the limitations of medical science. The reasonable patient will expect his doctor to be neither omnipotent nor omniscient. It is likely that this assumption on behalf of the patient – that his doctor is omnipotent – contributes to many of the instances where patients seek help from their doctors for what are, strictly speaking, non-medical problems. This assumption of omnipotence is naturally very flattering to the doctor, and a bad doctor may respond to it by thinking that his competence and power extend into areas where in fact they do not. Thus he may be led to offer authoritative advice about problems (moral, personal or emotional) on which as a medical practitioner he is not an expert. He may also be led to prescribe medicines for conditions which are beyond the scope of medicine to treat. Rightly or wrongly, it has become a commonplace that stimulant and tranquillising drugs are abused in this way. If abuse of this sort does occur, part of the blame must fall upon patients who go to a doctor with the false expectation that simply because he is a doctor he will have an answer and a treatment for everything.

It must be said that one cannot always draw a sharp line between medical and non-medical problems. A patient may come to a doctor with physical symptoms which in fact have their origin in some personal or psychological problem. The doctor may be required to offer advice about non-medical matters if he is to treat the patient's physical symptoms. A good doctor will know when he is faced with a personal problem about which he can advise the patient himself and when he is faced with a more serious kind of problem which needs to be referred to a trained psychiatrist or some other specialist adviser. Because physical symptoms can have their origin in psychological and personal problems, one needs to qualify the blunt insistence that patients should not seek non-medical advice from their doctors.

It would in any case be wrong to say that a patient should never go to his doctor seeking advice or help on personal problems. Many people in the course of time build up a strong relationship with their general practitioner and he may become a family friend. Thus in some cases he may be consulted about problems which are definitely non-medical. But insofar as he does give advice on non-medical matters it is as a friend, not as a physician. Any authority his advice may have does not derive from the medical qualifications he holds but from his position as a trusted confidant. This is not to suggest, however, that a patient's proper expectations of a doctor will not encourage him to regard his doctor as a confidant.

Many factors may contribute to a doctor's attaining such a position of trust with his patients, not least the length of time they have been in his charge. But it is clear that a patient's readiness to offer confidences to his doctor might reflect the high moral expectations that many have of their doctors. It would be too simple to say that patients expect their doctors to be wise and good just because they are doctors. But one can say that medicine is regarded as a vocation, and a vocation that is directed towards noble ends. Thus members of the medical profession are often held in high moral esteem. Patients do expect that doctors should regard medicine as a vocation and not simply as a means of earning a living. This sense of vocation that many doctors in fact have can, of course, be abused. It will be the bad patient who expects his doctor to be at his beck and call at all times. If society expects doctors to have a sense of vocation, it has a corresponding duty to see that they are adequately remunerated and that there are enough doctors to allow them reasonable hours of work. Nonetheless we do expect that doctors will have a basic altruism. This can perhaps be formulated in the following way: we expect a good doctor to regard a patient's being ill as a sufficient reason for treating him.

Doctors may fight shy of these high moral expectations but they seem unavoidable. We cannot think of medicine as just another job because in the first instance the concept of health is one with deeply favourable evaluative overtones. We are thus bound to look upon the office of restoring health as a noble one. Furthermore, a doctor can expect to face difficult and agonising questions in the course of his duties, questions on which lives will depend. Someone lacking a basic degree of charity, courage and practical wisdom will be unable to carry out such duties properly. One should not, of course, sentimentalise the profession and ignore the fact that a great deal of a doctor's work may be routine; but at the same time the inevitability of these expectations must be recognised. When the patient goes to see the doctor, even if it is only about some minor matter, the doctor is in a position of trust; and this position of trust produces certain moral expectations. The high moral expectations which patients can have of their doctors are strikingly illustrated by the portraits of doctors in works of literature: for example, the figure of Alan Woodcourt in Dickens's *Bleak House*.

I have indicated that there is another side to this coin, that is, that the expectation that doctors will have a sense of vocation entails corresponding duties on the part of the patients and society. These moral expectations also entail that a doctor's conscience must be respected by his patients and thus that they cannot properly expect him to do things which go against his conscience. For in a way I have been arguing that some of the important qualities which go to make a good doctor are qualities which help to make a good man. The doctor cannot be expected to have a basic charity and practical wisdom and yet to do things which go against these merely because the patient demands them.

I introduced these considerations by way of the point that patients may come to treat their doctor as a trusted confidant. By no means all patients will come to have so good a relationship with their doctor, but it does seem reasonable for patients generally to expect their doctors to offer them a genuine adult relationship. This entails two things. First, patients can reasonably expect to be listened to. Secondly, they can expect to have the nature of their condition and any treatment that they are undergoing explained to them. We are talking here of the ideal case. The patient may forfeit the first right if he is so garrulous or hypochondriac as to make serious and unjustified inroads into the doctor's limited time. Such a patient may not deserve a proper hearing and may rightly expect to be treated briskly. A patient may be so foolish or excitable as to make it impossible to explain to him properly the nature of his condition. These sorts of cases, however, are ones in which the proper relationship between patient and doctor cannot be maintained. Where the relationship is working properly the patient can expect to be heard and to be told what is wrong with him. The relationship may break down because of faults on either side, but the doctor can be expected to make a reasonable effort to listen and to explain.

The patient's expectation that he will be told the truth about his condition is a particularly important one. There is a temptation in the case of serious illness to hide the truth from the patient. I am arguing that the patient may reasonably expect his doctor to resist this temptation. The doctor may, of course, have to conceal or mask diagnosis because the patient is unable to respond to it properly. Where a patient probably has only a minor complaint but may possibly have something more serious, the doctor may have to conceal part of his diagnosis because he judges the patient to be incapable of appreciating the balance of probabilities: panic and despondency will set in should the serious condition ever be mentioned; hence the strong motive for concealment.

The reasonable patient can, however, expect to be told the truth. His expectation is grounded first of all in the presumption that he will be treated like an adult and that an adult relationship between doctor and patient will be possible only when truth-telling is the norm. Truthfulness is in any case a virtue and one should expect to tell the truth unless there are overriding reasons for not doing so. One of the reasons why truthfulness is a virtue is that men have found that it is a quality generally needed if they are successfully to carry out cooperative ventures together. Now, in many non-surgical cases the treatment of illness is just such a cooperative venture. The course of treatment may extend over a period of time and during that time the extensive cooperation of the patient may be required, for example in the taking of medicines at prescribed times or in the following of a special diet. It will usually be easier to secure this cooperation if the patient knows what is wrong with him and how his treatment is related to his condition. It is known that millions of pounds worth of medicine prescribed by doctors go unused each year. Whilst some of this waste is no doubt due solely to the stupidity or cussedness of patients, at least some of it may be partly due to a failure on the doctor's part properly to explain the nature of the patient's condition and how his treatment relates to it. If patients do not feel that they have been listened to properly or that they have been told the truth, they may lose confidence in their doctor and thus fail to carry out his instructions.

The cooperative nature of the doctor-patient relationship cannot be stressed too strongly. There are some surgical cases (that is, those involving sudden emergencies or accidents) where the doctor and patient do not converse until treatment is over. But in the vast majority of cases the doctor will need the patient's own account of his symptoms before treatment, and the patient's cooperation during it. As with any other adult relationship the doctor-patient relationship must be founded upon mutual trust and confidence if it is to be successful. This entails truthfulness on both sides. It also means that the parties must come to the relationship with the right expectations, that is with expectations that are mutually acceptable. Misunderstanding and conflict may arise if the patient has expectations that his doctor cannot or will not meet. This is to underline again the importance of the question before us.

References

1 Markillie, R E D. Difficult patients and difficult doctors. In: Melinsky, M A H. ed. *Religion and medicine.* London, SCM Press, 1970. p 79.

3

THE DOCTOR'S DUTY TO HEAL AND THE PATIENT'S CONSENT IN THE JEWISH TRADITION

Immanuel Jakobovits

In Jewish thought and law, human life enjoys an absolute, intrinsic and infinite value. Man is not the owner of his body but merely its custodian, charged to preserve it from any physical harm and to promote its health where this has been impaired.

This principle has both positive and negative applications. It turns healing where necessary into a religious duty, devolving on patient and doctor alike. Conversely, neither patient nor doctor has the right to refuse receiving or rendering such medical aid as is essential for the preservation of life and health. This principle therefore overrides such personal freedoms as may conflict with it, just as the obligation to prevent a suicide (or murder) attempt, by force if necessary, annuls the right or freedom to choose (or inflict) death. Again, innocent life is not ours that we can dispose of it, and where the individual may wish to surrender it, society or any member of it becomes obligated to frustrate any act – by commission or omission – of self-destruction.

Only in two rather marginal cases may the duty to preserve life, or not to risk it, require some qualification. Unavoidable risks may obviously be taken in medical or surgical procedures which are tried and generally accepted. Where no known cures are applicable, experimental or doubtful treatments may be applied in a desperate gamble to save life, even if the chances of success are less than even, provided that such treatments are administered solely for the benefit of the patient and not simply for research purposes. Jewish law also permits the use of analgesics to relieve extreme suffering in terminally-ill patients, even when there is some risk that they may prove fatal, so long as such consequences are entirely unintended and the sole purpose is to relieve pain, not to shorten life.

Secondly, while any form of direct euthanasia, under whatever circumstances, is branded as murder and can never be sanctioned, with or without the patient's consent, some Rabbinic authorities hold that the doctor's obligation stops short of requiring him to sustain a lingering life in its final stage by *artificial* means. In other words, where there is no hope of any recovery and continued or renewed treatment would only serve to prolong the dying agony, the doctor may be allowed to let nature take its course and to suspend medical or surgical treatments as well as resuscitation by machines, provided he takes no *action* whatever to induce death and he does not deprive the patient of *natural* means of subsistence, such as food. ('Action' would include switching off, as distinct from not applying, an artificial respirator.) But these strictly-confined exceptions apart, doctors and patients alike are obligated to preserve life, whatever their personal preference.

On the other hand, out of respect for his dignity and to encourage his cooperation, a patient is entitled to be informed of any treatment to be given him, so long as such information is calculated to help the patient. It should be withheld or modified only if there are well-grounded risks that, far from helping him, it would be liable to damage his interests, either mentally by his fear of the prospect of the treatment, or physically by inducing him to resist the treatment. For the same reason, a patient should be informed of a fatal prognosis only if one is reasonably certain that by revealing his condition he will not suffer a serious physical or mental setback, notably by breaking his will to live and his confidence in recovery. In such cases, Jewish ethics would have no compunction in suppressing the truth from the patient or even in deceiving him. His well-being must be the primary consideration.

As a rule, the doctor's opinion – as that of the medical expert – takes precedence over any lay view, including the patient's. However, this rule is not absolute, since it operates only in favour of the patient's interests. The classic Jewish source for this rule is to be found in the detailed regulations on the Day of Atonement. Normally it is a grave offence to consume any food or drink throughout that 25-hour period, unless fasting would cause the slightest risk to life. Hence, if any competent doctor advises that the patient's condition requires him to eat, he is obliged to do so, even if he himself feels confident that he can fast without any hazard. On the other hand, once a patient himself feels that he cannot fast without risk, his opinion must be respected in his favour, and food must be served to him even if a hundred doctors unanimously say otherwise. This rule is derived from the verse: 'The heart knoweth its own bitterness' (Proverbs 14:10). In other words, in regard to anything required by the patient, his own assessment of his needs is supreme and overrides any medical opinion, even if this judgment involves what would otherwise be a grave religious violation. But in the reverse circumstances, when medical opinion requires a possibly life-saving action not deemed necessary, or rejected, by the patient, his wishes must be disregarded, even at the cost of his spiritual ideals (for example, his desire to fast on the Day of Atonement) and *a fortiori* his physical considerations (for example, the desire to avoid the pain of surgery or the crippling effects of an amputation essential to save his life).

This modification of the general rule, giving the patient certain limited rights to overrule the doctor, implies that there is at least some residual claim to consent in favour of the patient. In black-and-white cases, where medical experience clearly sets the need for treatment at a maximum and the risk factor at a minimum, the general rule operates without reservation, and the patient need not be consulted (though he should be informed under the above-mentioned conditions), since his wishes or consent are irrelevant to the overriding duty to save his life. But the modification of the rule is weighty enough to take the patient's wishes into account when we deal with grey areas where the prospects of success are reduced and the chances of failure increased. The distinction here is not between 'ordinary' and 'extraordinary' treatments, but between procedures liable to be more or less effective, such as high-risk, experimental or controversial treatments.

In theory, once the patient's own views have to be disregarded, even force if necessary would have to be applied to protect his life – or even his health, which one is equally obligated to preserve. But in practice, and bearing in mind that there are never black-and-white situations in medicine, leaving no room for some doubts or risks, all the judgments are bound to be sufficiently relative to exclude the use of force and to allow for some distinction between life and health. The line obviously cannot be drawn with absolute precision, especially since many a health hazard may lead to some eventual risk to life. There must therefore remain some element of subjectivity in judging the extent to which a patient's refusal to give consent should be considered in individual cases. Nevertheless, the above principles and directives of Jewish law and ethics are sufficiently well-defined to serve as general guidelines.

They may be summed up as follows:

1 It is a religious obligation to protect human life and health, incumbent upon a doctor as upon any other person in a position to do so.
2 The duty to preserve life and not to risk it can be modified only for high-risk treatments where no known cures exist, for administering possibly fatal pain-killers for the sole purpose of relieving suffering, and for the suspension of treatments serving only to prolong the dying agony.
3 A doctor is never morally entitled to withhold or withdraw his services, whether or not a contractual relationship* exists between him and his patient, unless a more competent doctor is available. A refusal to render medical aid where required is deemed as tantamount to bloodshed.
4 A patient has no right to refuse medical treatment deemed essential by competent medical opinion for the preserva-

* That is, a relationship in which consent has been given or could be presumed from the patient's engaging a doctor to look after his health. Difficulties over the word 'contract' are recognised, but not pursued here.

tion of his life or health, and his consent need not be procured for such treatment.

5 In the discharge of the doctor's obligation to save life and limb, and in the absence of the patient's consent, the doctor may even be required to expose himself to the risk of legal claims for unauthorised assault and battery.

6 A fatal diagnosis should never be divulged to the patient unless the doctor and/or family are reasonably confident that, far from causing mental anguish or a physical set-back, such information is likely to relieve the patient through the knowledge that his suffering is coming to an end.

7 While the patient should always be informed of treatments or procedures to be applied, both as a matter of respecting his rights and to secure his cooperation, his prior consent is required, and should be sought, only in cases of high-risk treatments or doubtful or experimental cures, or differences of opinion among equally competent medical experts.

8 The onus of choosing between various alternative forms of treatment, or none at all, rests upon the doctor, and patients should never be expected to render what are essentially purely medical decisions.

4

CONSENT AND PRACTICE IN THE CATHOLIC TRADITION

Brendan Soane

Sometimes it happens that a doctor and his patient disagree about treatment, the patient not wanting to undergo the treatment recommended by the doctor, or wanting a treatment which the doctor does not recommend. This paper explores such occasions and attempts to apportion responsibility between the parties.

It is accepted in the Catholic tradition that the final decision about what treatment will be given will be shared by doctor and patient. A doctor cannot be obliged morally to provide a treatment of which he disapproves, for medical or moral reasons, and a patient is not obliged to accept a treatment simply because a doctor recommends it. This accords with the custom of obtaining consent which is followed in British medical practice. It also accords with the Catholic understanding of the respect due to the freedom and dignity of the person. Typical of this understanding is St John Damascene, who taught that man is said to be made in the image of God inasmuch as he is intelligent, free to judge, and a master of himself. So far as possible individuals should make decisions which concern their own life and its circumstances. To deny them this right is to ignore their natural dignity. So patients should not be asked to abrogate their right to decide issues which affect them deeply; but neither, on the other hand, should doctors be so asked.

The human person has freedom of choice, but he cannot claim the absolute freedom of God. He is created and sustained by God, and will find his final end in communion with God. He must direct his life with this end in view. This he will do if he ensures that his free choices conform to the will of God, whether expressed in the general moral order or in personal vocation. The difficulty in many medical choices is to know what is the will of God. A few comments on discovering the will of God may be in order.

The Christian moral law is not primarily a written law; it is a law of grace. We believe that the Holy Spirit of God is active in the souls of good people to purify and elevate their minds, their wills, and, ultimately, their whole way of life. However the Holy Spirit does not usually by-pass ordinary processes of moral decision. So the Christian who has a moral decision to make must take counsel, consider carefully, and decide prudently what should be done. He will consider the facts of the case and the possible outcome of different courses of action, and he will make a judgment in accordance with sound moral principles.

Let us now consider the Christian patient. Among those from whom he will take counsel are doctors and representatives of the Church, although he would probably only consult the latter if the decision seemed to have serious moral implications. From doctors he will expect information about his state of health and a recommendation about the treatment which is most suitable. If the matter is important he may consult another doctor. To treat the information and judgment of these experts lightly would be extremely imprudent and, by that fact, would be immoral. However the patient is not obliged to follow his doctor's recommendations, for it is his own responsibility to make decisions concerning his own future. What he should do is give their recommendations serious attention.

From representatives of the Church the Christian patient or doctor will expect guidance about Christian moral principles. But not all guidance is given with the same degree of authority. The Church teaches a message of salvation attuned to the conditions of life. This message includes both a body of dogma and more specific moral guidance. It is believed by Roman Catholics that the body of dogma can be proclaimed infallibly. On moral matters it includes only the most basic moral principles, such as the command to love God and neighbour, and the right to life. More specific guidance results from shared experience and co-reflection in the light of the basic moral principles and is capable of development and reform. Even teachings which fall within this latter category should be treated with the utmost respect, and should normally, when they emanate from those whose position in the Church gives them authority to teach, be accepted and obeyed. But, because of their essentially reformable character, it can happen that a well-informed and competent Roman Catholic might, after careful consideration, come to a different conclusion. Such a person is free to follow his own judgment, although he should not close his mind to the possibility of being wrong.

Authoritative moral teaching is always general and belongs to the speculative order. The individual has to decide in practice what he ought to do. This decision will be made, not only in the light of authoritative guidance, but also with due regard for circumstances of person, time and place. Only the individual and his personal counsellors will know what these are. Therefore guidance offered to the whole Church does not preempt personal decision about what should be done in the here and now in the service of God.

The teaching and opinions of theologians are also a most important guide to moral principles, as are the opinions of other Christians and of all people of good will.

A responsible decision must also take account of the civil law. The Catholic tradition recognises in civil law a moral authority, that is, a claim on conscience, when it satisfies certain conditions. These require that it be promulgated by lawful authority and be designed to secure the common good. A law which does not conform with sound moral principles has no authority as law and no claim on conscience, although, if he can do so without infringing moral law himself, a Christian would normally obey it in the interest of peace, and from respect for authority. An example might be willingness to obey an excessive tax demand. That the civil law permits an action which a Christian might judge was contrary to moral law does not free him from his obligation to respect moral law. So, for example, a Christian might judge that it would be immoral to perform an abortion. The fact that the abortion would be permitted by civil law, or even commanded, would not free him from his obligation to observe moral law.

Now let us apply these general principles to the doctor and the patient. The doctor must make up his mind about what treatments he may licitly apply. Among those which he thinks morally unobjectionable, which would normally include most of those in common use, he must in a particular case decide which offers the best chance of success. This he will recommend to the patient. It is, in the last analysis, for the patient to decide if he is willing to accept a particular treatment. The doctor must respect his wishes even if he thinks them irresponsible. If the patient wants a treatment which the doctor thinks inadvisable there can be no obligation on the doctor to provide it, and he certainly should not do so if it offends his own moral beliefs. The patient may not require the doctor to do anything which offends against the doctor's conscience, but neither may he accept any treatment which offends against his own, however strongly the doctor might recommend it.

All of this assumes that the patient is an adult in full possession of his faculties. Children and adults who are unconscious, semi-conscious or mentally subnormal or incompetent, cannot give true fully informed consent. So far as possible their wishes should be respected, but usually others must decide on their behalf what treatment will be accepted. Catholic teaching states that the support of children is a right primarily of parents, so they are the proper persons from whom consent should be sought for the treatment of children. If they judge that a treatment is not in the best interests of their child, then they are entitled to refuse it on the child's behalf. Likewise, in a nation where financial assistance is unavailable, they might licitly refuse even life-saving treatments if they judged that they could not afford to pay for them.

Parental authority is to be understood as in the service of the child and is to be used in the child's best interests. It is not an absolute authority. It could happen that a doctor thinks that parents are acting against the best interests of their child. If he thinks that the refusal to allow treatment is a danger to the life or well-being of the child he could be morally obliged to seek the intervention of the civil authorities.* In this context Bernard Häring, a German moral theologian, discusses a case where parents refuse a blood transfusion which would save the life of their child. He accepts that a doctor would have recourse to the civil authorities. If there is no legislation he suggests that the doctor will do all he can to save the life of the child. He adds, 'However, when legislation stipulates that the physician must follow the dictates of the family, he will not always be empowered to perform the transfusion.'[2]

There does not seem to be any agreed body of teaching by Catholic authors on who has final responsibility for deciding whether or not to treat an unconscious or mentally defective adult. It is presumed that near relatives, husband or wife, parents, brothers or sisters, and so on, will be consulted, and consent would normally be sought from them. They should decide in the light of the presumed wishes of the patient, which may sometimes be known because he gave expression to a considered choice when he was competent to do so. If his wishes cannot be known, they must decide in his presumed best interests. If they can come to no decision then the doctors must decide on behalf of the patient. It is possible that a doctor's professional standards might dictate that he does not accede to a request to terminate treatment. It was this that happened in the famous case of Karen Quinlan. Her parents requested the doctors to switch off a respirator and they refused to do so until instructed by a court of law. (Even then the patient did not die; her vital functions persisted without respirator support.)

Before I conclude it might be useful if I said something about the teaching of Catholic authors on the obligation to accept treatment designed to save life.

The teaching distinguishes between ordinary and extraor-

* See *The Times* Law Report, 8 August 1981, Re 'B' (Minor). The Court of Appeal authorised an operation on a child whom a Local Authority had made a ward of court when the parents refused consent to an operation which the doctors regarded as normal and in the child's interest.

dinary means of saving life. The words are misleading unless it is realised that they have a specialised meaning.

Ordinary means of preserving life include all medicines, treatments and operations which offer a reasonable hope of benefit to the patient, and which can be obtained and used without excessive expense, pain or other inconvenience.

Extraordinary means of preserving life are all medicines, treatments and operations which cannot be obtained without excessive expense, pain or other inconvenience, or which, if used, would not offer a reasonable hope of benefit.

It is generally taught that an individual has an obligation to accept ordinary means of saving his life. He has no obligation to accept extraordinary means, although he may do so if he wishes. Exceptional circumstances might make acceptance of extraordinary means morally obligatory, for example, the need to settle important affairs, whether temporal or spiritual, or special responsibilities.[1]

The application of these principles is discussed in most Catholic works on medical ethics (for example, *Euthanasia and Clinical Practice*[3]). It is sufficient to note here that the judgment about whether a means is to be defined as ordinary or extraordinary in a particular case will depend on circumstances of time and place, on the personal qualities of the patient, such as age, general state of mind and health and so on, on the hope of benefit, and even on such subjective factors as whether an individual thinks life would be worth living in the circumstances brought about by the treatment. A doctor can best appreciate the objective factors, but only the patient can appreciate the subjective ones.

As was stated above, the decision whether or not to accept treatment rests with the patient, unless he is an infant or incompetent to make it. Naturally it will be made in the closest possible consultation with the doctors. In many cases others, such as trusted relatives, ministers of religion and respected friends, will be consulted. If the patient judges that he is obliged to accept a particular treatment in accordance with moral law, then the doctor is morally obliged to grant it (with the provisos above about the conscience of the doctor). If the patient wishes to undergo an extraordinary treatment, unless the wish is unreasonable, relatives and doctors should accede to the request. If the doctor must make the decision, for example in an emergency, or when the patient is incapable and there are no relatives available to consult, then, according to the authorities whom I have consulted, he will not merely seek to determine what is ordinary and extraordinary, he will use every means of saving life which he has at his disposal and which offers a reasonable hope of success. In other words, he will give the benefit of any doubt to saving life. This ideal is thought to be important for medical progress and to prevent a euthanasian mentality. It would hardly be just to press it to the point where it imposed intolerable burdens on patients or relatives.

The reasoning behind the moral teaching on ordinary and extraordinary means of saving life (that is, obligatory and voluntary means) depends first on the belief that we have a duty to God to conserve and protect our lives. It depends next on the belief that positive duties can be overridden by other claims, and that moral impotence can excuse from observance of the positive moral law in some cases. Moral impotence occurs when a duty which is prescribed, for example, taking measures to preserve one's life or health, cannot be carried out without extraordinary effort or the risk of grave harm. (It is distinguished from physical impotence, which means that it simply cannot be carried out at all because the subject lacks the ability or the instruments.) God is not thought to command the morally impossible except in special cases; for example, a doctor might be obliged to risk his life by staying in a plague-ridden city to provide essential help. The teaching rests on the further belief that nobody can be morally obliged to do what is useless; so a proposed treatment must offer a real hope of benefit to the patient.

There is a subjective element in the determination of what counts as morally impossible and, therefore, extraordinary, because what requires a great effort on the part of one person, or would entail risk of great harm, may be easier to achieve or less risky for another. Likewise a treatment might offer a real hope of benefit to one person but not to another, because the circumstances of their lives differ. Nevertheless there is an objective element. Not just anything can be said to satisfy the criteria for extraordinary treatments. The more common medical treatments could only be considered extraordinary in special cases, and anyone who refused common life-saving procedures would normally do so because he did not sufficiently value his life.

I am conscious that in this paper I might seem to have undervalued the role of the doctor in making decisions. In fact his position is crucial. What is asked of him is that he make his recommendations in such a way that the patient is helped to give a free and informed consent, and if he should refuse consent, that he knows what he is doing. What the doctor says and how he says it will often sway a decision one way or another. He should value the consent of the patient, because it is in our consenting and refusing consent to one or another course of action that our whole dignity as free persons is manifested.

References

1 Duncan, A S and others. eds. *Dictionary of medical ethics.* Revised edition. London, Darton, Longman and Todd; New York, Crossroad, 1981. pp 315, 266.

2 Häring, B. *Medical ethics.* Slough, St Paul Publications, 1972. p 40.

3 Linacre Centre. *Euthanasia and clinical practice: trends, principles and alternatives* (part 3). The report of a working party. London, Linacre Centre, 1982.

5

DIVERGENCE ON CONSENT: A PHILOSOPHICAL ASSAY

Peter Byrne

There are a number of reasons why consent has become an important topic in medical debates during recent years. One reason has undoubtedly been provided by the law. In an increasingly litigious society self-interest alone dictates that doctors be concerned with issues of consent. Perhaps some doctors would like to discuss consent in medical practice solely with this legal aspect in mind, concentrating upon what the doctor must do if he is to keep himself out of the courts. A severely pragmatic discussion of this sort would aim to avoid raising questions about the fundamental moral principles which ought to govern the doctor-patient relationship. One of the reasons why such a discussion would be hopelessly limited is provided by the law itself: when we turn to the tradition of Anglo-American legal thinking on the question of consent we immediately find the clear presence of moral principle. Leaving aside certain special cases, Anglo-American common law gives no right to qualified medical practitioners to interfere with a person's body without his consent. This point remains unaffected even where such interference is well-intentioned or is actually beneficial to the patient. Such well-intentioned, but uninvited, interference renders the medical practitioner liable to a civil claim for damages or to a criminal prosecution for assault. This seems to me to say something very important about the inherent value of individual autonomy even where interfering with this autonomy is otherwise beneficial. So we cannot escape moral issues by retreating to the law. All must accept that there are important moral principles relevant to issues of consent and that the doctor's approach to these issues will be the better if it is based upon an awareness of principle and not simply upon expediency. It is the merit of the papers by the Chief Rabbi and Fr Brendan Soane that they so clearly highlight the principles involved. With admirable lucidity and precision they introduce us to the teachings of two major religious traditions which have profoundly influenced Western attitudes to these issues. My main aim will be to show how their contributions help us in thinking about the principles governing consent. I shall focus on the areas of agreement and disagreement between them and indicate, insofar as I can, the reasons behind the disagreements. Finally, I shall develop some thoughts of my own on this topic, drawing upon a common philosophical inheritance.

In thinking about consent in medical practice it is necessary to distinguish clearly two viewpoints: that of the doctor and that of the patient. We must consider how far the doctor is obliged to consult and inform the patient before treatment and how far the patient is obliged to accept the doctor's advice, once consulted and informed. Consideration of these questions must take into account another distinction, that between treatments deemed necessary to save life and those necessary merely to restore health or vigour. As the Chief Rabbi notes in his paper, this is not a precise distinction, but it must be borne in mind when considering the obligations which fall upon doctor and patient. One may not be able to draw it in all cases, but we can see that it is nonetheless a real distinction when we reflect that some men may live for a very long time with ill-health or with some bodily function maimed or impaired. Distinguishing these two viewpoints and two types of treatment, it may be seen that there are at least four questions which can be raised concerning consent and practice. They are:

1 In the case of treatment deemed life-saving, is the doctor obliged to consult the patient before starting treatment?
2 In the case of treatment deemed life-saving, is the patient obliged to accept the doctor's advice?
3 In the case of treatment not deemed life-saving, is the doctor obliged to consult the patient before starting treatment?

4 In the case of treatment not deemed life-saving, is the patient obliged to accept the doctor's advice?

The identification of these questions provides a means of comparing our authors' views. I begin with questions 2 and 4 and the patient's obligation to accept his doctor's advice.

Regarding 2, it seems to be the clear teaching of the Jewish tradition that the patient is obliged to undergo any treatment a competent medical practitioner deems necessary to save his life. By the same token, Fr Soane affirms: 'It is generally taught that an individual has an obligation to accept ordinary means of saving his life'. The distinction between ordinary and extraordinary means implicitly drawn in this quotation is not one that the Chief Rabbi finds wholly acceptable. But despite this difference both our authors recognise that patients are generally obliged to agree to treatments deemed life-saving. The Chief Rabbi gives one justification for this obligation most clearly in his opening paragraph: a man's life is not his own to give up or dispose of. There is in his second paragraph an implicit assimilation of a refusal to accept treatment to an act of suicide; and suicide is accounted a sin in both traditions, the Jewish and the Roman Catholic.

As I indicated above, this measure of agreement is not complete. According to the Chief Rabbi, the patient may escape his obligation to accept life-saving treatments only when these involve high risk, or are experimental or controversial. Such treatments would be included in Fr Soane's category of 'extraordinary means'. They would come under the heading of those which 'would not offer a reasonable hope of benefit'. But this phrase refers only to some of the features Fr Soane would allow as making a treatment extraordinary. Thus he lists 'treatments and operations which cannot be obtained without excessive expense, pain or other inconvenience', and he affirms that a treatment's being extraordinary could depend 'on such subjective factors as whether an individual thinks life would be worth living in the circumstances brought about by the treatment'. I take it that none of the factors referred to here would provide a sound reason in the Jewish tradition for regarding life-saving treatment as elective; for the God-given character of life is seen as placing us under an absolute obligation to preserve it. The patient is to confine himself to the question of whether the treatment proposed really does offer a reasonable hope of saving life; if it does, he is obliged to accept it. This indicates that the freedom of decision given to the patient in these circumstances by the Jewish tradition is a somewhat restricted one. For the factors which might justify a patient in refusing treatment are matters for *medical* judgment and the patient can surely be allowed little freedom of decision on this view once he has placed himself in the hands of a competent medical practitioner whose judgment is respected by his colleagues. The only case would be where his doctors acknowledged an extraordinary risk and asked the patient if he were prepared to take it. Fr Soane, however, affirms that it is for both doctor *and* patient to decide whether a treatment is extraordinary. This reflects what is for him an important principle: 'the final decision about what treatment will be given is shared by doctor and patient'.

I find difficulties in both these divergent positions. The Chief Rabbi's position raises the following problem. His affirmation that the patient has no choice but to accept life-saving treatment is linked with the claim that, because human life is God-given, it enjoys 'an absolute, intrinsic and infinite value'. I am not entirely clear as to the meaning of this key assertion, but if it is to produce the desired consequence of limiting the patient's right to refuse treatment, it seems that it must be read as claiming that the preservation or protection of life is a goal of action before which all others are subordinate. Everything must give way to this goal. But when so read, this principle seems to me to be false and I think that many people would agree with me. There are several types of occasion in which men sacrifice their lives for something where I and others would *praise* them. Furthermore, men engage in numerous types of activity in which they knowingly or willingly put their lives at great risk. I do not feel obliged forcefully to restrain my neighbour from engaging in a hazardous occupation or sport. I might even look up to him. I do not think that human life has infinite value in exactly the sense which the Chief Rabbi's argument seems to require. So where it is the case that the acceptance of life-saving treatment would conflict with other interests and goals of the patient, it does not seem to me that the apparently simple thought that life has infinite value necessarily settles the question and obliges the patient always to follow his doctor's advice. I think that common opinion in the West would be closer to Fr Soane's judgment in these matters than to the Chief Rabbi's. As I shall explain below, this in part reflects the extent to which Western thought has been influenced by moral traditions distinct from Judaism.

The difficulty to be seen in Fr Soane's position stems from his willingness to accept such a broad range of factors as making life-saving treatment extraordinary and thus elective. The reference to 'such subjective factors as whether life would be worth living in the circumstances brought about by treatment' allows of a wide interpretation. For example, a patient might not be under an obligation to move to a different part of the world, even if a change of climate was deemed to be the only means of saving his life. One problem here is that the more subjective factors we allow as making a treatment extraordinary, as the moralist sees it, the less it will mean to say that patients are *obliged* to accept ordinary means of saving their lives. Whilst it is clear that Fr Soane does not wish to say that a patient could refuse life-saving treatment on the basis of a mere whim, he does want to say that a patient is not obliged to choose life if the effort of so doing would be too great for him. Yet despite this Fr Soane writes that 'we have a duty to God to conserve and protect our lives'. This duty can only be what moral philosophers call an 'imperfect duty'. Like, for example, the duty to help those in need, it requires judgment on the part of the individual to decide when and to what extent it should be acted upon. It may be set aside in particular cases in the light of other reasonable ends which the agent has. The Chief Rabbi's view, on the other hand, would be closer to the conclusion that the duty to conserve our lives is a 'perfect' one. A perfect duty demands unconditional observance on all occasions, and this, allowing for some exceptions in the treatment of the dying, is how the Chief Rabbi seems to regard the duty to conserve life.

We must note an important consequence of Fr Soane's belief that the duty to conserve our lives is an imperfect one. On Fr Soane's view, it cannot be the case that God's will is that we should always act to preserve our lives, come what may. On occasions it is right, and hence in accordance with the will of God, that we allow our physical existence to be curtailed rather than forsake other things or undergo great trials. If it be asked 'How then can suicide be wrong?' the answer (if indeed there is an answer) must be that the morally distinguishing feature of suicide lies in the fact that death results from a positive act rather than from a series of omissions. Only by stressing some such difference could we avoid the conclusion that suicide is sometimes morally justifiable.

Often a patient seeks advice and help from a doctor when his life is in no immediate danger. The treatment offered cannot be deemed life-saving. In this case is the patient obliged to accept medical advice? The Chief Rabbi's paper places the duty to preserve one's health on a par with that to preserve life. The patient then has no right to refuse medical treatment deemed essential to preserve his health. The Chief Rabbi, no doubt, wishes to allow exceptions here in the case of doubtful or experimental cures. Fr Soane, however, goes further than this and argues that, while he should not treat medical advice lightly, 'the patient is not obliged to follow his doctor's recommendations'.

Just as what was at issue in the discussion of life-saving treatment was how far a patient may judge other things to be more important than preserving his life, so here: could a patient rightfully regard some other good as more important than preserving or regaining his health? Suppose a patient be advised that the only way to recover health is by giving up his work, or is recommended a form of treatment which is extremely costly. The argument of Fr Soane's paper is that even if the doctor is right in thinking such measures essential to effect a recovery, it remains for the patient to decide whether good health is more important than his work, or is worth the cost of the recommended treatment. Statements in the Chief Rabbi's paper would seem to affirm that preserving health is an absolute obligation of the same sort as the absolute obligation to preserve life, and thus that nothing can be weighed against it. This is the crucial question. For if one admits that other things (one's work, the prosperity of one's family, and so on) could outweigh health, then it is clear that it is not for the doctor to decide when they do. To decide that a man can only recover his health if he changes his job is to make a medical decision; to decide that his health is more important than his work is not. If one allows that other things in the individual's life could outweigh his health, then it is clearly for him to decide when they do so (which is not to deny that others can have a say in the decision). One thinks here of the great men who have ruined their health in the cause of human progress. Such men are more commonly praised than blamed, thus testifying to the belief that health is not thought of as an absolute value. The common moral consciousness would thus seem closer to the Roman Catholic than to the Jewish view. And I think what has been said about sacrificing health in pursuit of some great good could also be said about life.

I have discussed the patient's obligation to accept medical advice before the doctor's obligation to inform and seek consent for a very good reason: the first issue is logically prior to the second. What view we take of the patient's obligation to accept advice will determine what view we take of the doctor's obligation to seek consent. If we believe that the patient has only a very limited right to refuse competent medical advice, we will believe that doctors have only a limited duty to seek consent: for in acting without prior consent, the doctor would not be violating the patient's right to decide to undergo treatment or not; the patient would have no right to refuse treatment if recommended by a competent medical practitioner. Correspondingly, if we urge that the patient has a real right to accept or refuse treatment, then we must insist that the doctor is duty-bound to consult him before proceeding. To do otherwise would be to violate one of the patient's essential rights. Thus it is that we see that the Chief Rabbi's paper heavily qualifies the doctor's duty to inform and seek consent, whilst Fr Soane's affirms it strongly.

Apart from cases involving experimental or high-risk treatments, the Chief Rabbi acknowledges no general obligation on the doctor to seek a patient's consent before treatment. His teaching would seem to draw no distinction between life-preserving and health-preserving treatments in this regard. He acknowledges a general obligation to *inform*, which he expresses thus: 'a patient is entitled to be informed of any treatment to be given him'. There might seem to be a contradiction here. For if in fact the doctor informs the patient beforehand of the treatment to be applied, is this not in practice to invite the patient's consent or refusal? However, the appearance of a contradiction is removed once we realise that information is to be given only if it is in the patient's interest. As I understand the argument, such information is not in the patient's interest if it will have the effect of inducing him to refuse treatment necessary to preserve his life or health. So information should not be given when there is a reasonable expectation that, once informed, the patient will refuse to undergo treatment. Leaving aside the exceptional cases of doubtful or experimental cures, information is not given with the aim of enabling the patient to exercise a decision to undergo or refuse treatment. In theory then, the patient's wishes (presumed or known) may be ignored according to this view. This is justified by the thought that the patient's 'well-being must be the primary consideration'. It may of course often be the case that the patient's well-being is promoted by circumventing his wishes. We may summarise the argument more formally in the following way. The obligation to inform the patient, arising out of the needs and demands of the doctor-patient relationship, is only a relative one. The doctor's obligation to restore health and save life is an absolute one. These two obligations can conflict and when they do the former must give way to the latter.

Fr Soane would dissent from this teaching. It is clear that, like the Chief Rabbi, he regards the doctor as justified in treating a patient without consultation where it is impossible to inform the patient beforehand (for example, when treating a comatose accident victim). But such exceptions do not conflict with the principle I see implicit in his paper: where at all possible a patient should always be consulted before treatment. Fr Soane would not allow the patient's wishes to be circumvented in the way the Chief Rabbi seems to envisage as possible. In the terminology used above, Fr Soane would deny that the doctor is under an absolute obligation to save life (or restore health), when this means that nothing can outweigh this obligation or limit its exercise. Catholic teaching is that the exercise of this obligation is limited by the rights of the patient: in this case his right as an adult human being to make decisions about his own life. The crucial sentences are these: 'As far as possible individuals should make decisions which concern their own life and its circumstances. To deny them this right is to ignore their natural dignity.'

The divergence of views we find here stems from a difference about the relative values of the goods secured through medical treatment (life, health) and human autonomy. Fr Soane's position rests on a recognition of the human capacity for self-direction and the consequent respect for the individual's will which results from this. This respect is one that all moralists will share. Where they will differ is over the weight to be given to it when it conflicts with the individual's own good or welfare. In some instances this respect may indeed lead to the agent's harm, because it will place limits on how far others may act paternalistically for his own good. To give a crude example, my bank manager may know better than I how my money should be managed: respect for my autonomy – entailing that I be consulted before decisions are made about my money – may on occasions be to my financial disadvantage. Perhaps what we have in this disagreement between our authors is another example of the recurrent debate about the limits of paternalism: how far may it be justified by the good it brings to its object? Respect for individual rights will place limits on paternalistic action. I do not suggest that the Jewish tradition depreciates such respect in general, but the limits on paternalism it promotes seem to be forsaken where health or life are at stake. The source of disagreement here lies in the fact that the Chief Rabbi seems to regard medical decisions bearing upon life and health as radically discontinuous with other decisions about a person's welfare. Fr Soane, on the other hand, sees a continuity: the normal restrictions on paternalism are extended, without misgiving, to medical care. Another mark of Fr Soane's belief that medical decisions are continuous with other decisions about welfare is found in his willingness to let factors like expense and personal inconvenience be weighed against the capacity of some treatment to save life.

We have looked at the measure of agreement and disagreement on the two pairs of questions I distinguished originally, relating to the patient's right to refuse treatment and the doctor's duty to consult. In both cases we see that the extent of disagreement between our authors stems from one source: a difference over the extent to which other things may be set alongside health and life. Are these strictly incommensurable with, because infinitely superior to, other aspects of a person's welfare? If they are not, then there is a valid area of decision-making in which the patient must share. He must be consulted by the doctor and have the final say in whether what is involved in treatment is worth the object (health or life) it is intended to secure.

The Jewish answer to the central question I pose here is clear: 'In Jewish thought and law, human life enjoys an absolute, intrinsic and infinite value.' It is this affirmation which introduces the key incommensurability of which I have written. But does this mean that those who deny this incommensurability think that life does not have an absolute, intrinsic and infinite value? Fr Soane and those who think like him are not necessarily committed to this negative view of the worth of human life. They must distinguish between the worth of a human being, which may be spoken of as absolute or intrinsic, and the worth of a human being's span of physical life. The second is not absolute and the high view taken of the worth of a human being may indeed dictate our taking a relative view of this. The example of allowing a dying patient 'a good death' may be used to illustrate this distinction. Because of the value we place upon the individual human being, out of respect for his worth as a person, we may not act so as to extend his physical existence as long as it is humanly possible and at all costs. This distinction between the worth of the human being and the worth of a human being's physical existence has its origins, I believe, in the tradition of classical philosophy of which Roman Catholicism is one heir. This tradition allows for a relative view of physical existence because of the intrinsic worth it sees in the human person. Perhaps the most famous illustration of this is the death of Socrates (as recorded in Plato's *Crito* and *Phaedo*): Socrates dies willingly cooperating with the sentence of the court, while those around him urge that he escape the sentence of the law, but he would rather die than live dishonoured. The Jewish and Catholic views differ where they do on account of the influence of this classical tradition.

This distinction between the worth of the person and the worth of his physical existence can be, and has been, taken to the extreme whereby man's physical existence is actually denigrated. The West perhaps owes in large measure the high value it places upon physical existence to Judaism. This tradition has centrally maintained that man's existence is an historical embodied one. If we take this thought seriously, then the high value we place upon human beings must be reflected in the value we place upon the life and health of the body. We must regard these as precious and therefore not to be thrown away lightly. All that our distinction between the worth of persons and the worth of physical existence allows is that in some cases, necessarily few, we may place life and health second to other aims we have. It is obvious that the Western moral consciousness has been influenced by the classical tradition I have described. Many would recognise that there are limits to the pursuit of health and life. They would indeed read the account of Socrates' death as Plato intended it to be read, namely as a description of a noble, meritorious act.

To return finally to the question of consent in medical

practice, we must ask why it is we accord an intrinsic worth to human beings. Part of the answer must surely make reference to human autonomy – that capacity for self-direction which has been mentioned already. If we respect this capacity, we see why it is that doctors should seek consent where at all possible. The patient's status as an autonomous human being, master of his own life, is denigrated otherwise. It is in this respect for autonomy that the basis for a principled attitude towards consent lies.

6

THE DEVELOPMENT OF THE CONCEPTS AND PRACTICE OF PATIENT CONSENT

Paul E Polani

Introduction

'Consent' is defined in a number of ways. It means compliance or approval, especially of what is done or proposed by another. It signifies capable, deliberate, and voluntary agreement to, or concurrence in, some act or purpose implying physical and mental power and free actions. In the Compact Edition of the *Oxford English Dictionary*, consent is defined as 'voluntary agreement to, or acquiescence in, what another proposes or desires; compliance, concurrence, permission'.* It is not immediately clear that the word *per se* implies knowledge and understanding of what is done or proposed, so that the word 'informed' is used to clarify the last-named points. Legally, according to a statement from the USA, the doctrine that 'a consent effective as authority to form therapy can arise only from the patient's understanding of alternatives to and risks of the therapy' is commonly denominated 'informed consent'. The same appellation is frequently assigned to the doctrine requiring physicians, as a matter of duty to patients, to communicate information as to such alternatives and risks.**[29]

There are many aspects of medical work to which the problems of consent and informed consent apply. Thus even the touching of a patient by a doctor requires consent: the

* The word is used in political theory to signify voluntary agreement by a people to organise a civil society and give authority to the government (and the people as a whole are sovereign).

** Notes on Judge Spotswood W Robinson III's opinion, delivered in *Canterbury v Spence* [US Court of Appeals, District of Columbia Circuit, 19 May 1972. 464 *Federal Reporter*, 2nd series, 772].

act, in its absence, may be taken in law to constitute assault. Informed consent is especially relevant to two aspects of medical work, treatment and research. These are by no means always as clearly distinguishable as they might seem at first glance to be.

There is little doubt that the issue of informed consent and the discussions and deliberations about it, especially in relation to human experimentation, are derived from the Nuremberg Trials, and the codified declaration that followed the Trials in 1947. The Code was drafted by the Judicial Tribunal, with the help of medical experts, and sets out ten basic principles or standards, to which physicians must conform with regard to experiments on human subjects[25,44] (see also Appendix A). But there are also many facets – or, perhaps, all – of medical treatment that involve the issue of informed consent, which is one that is a key practical and ethical consideration in medicine. The following notes are an attempt to review the origins of consent with regard to medical praxis.

Medical etiquette and ethics in history

GREECE AND ROME

A summary statement is that consent, specifically, was not considered an integral part of the patient-doctor relationship, or partnership, until very recent times. Nevertheless, it is interesting to look at this relationship in closer detail, and at the general ethical content of medicine from this particular standpoint, from antiquity to modern times.

In a general sense, in ancient times, there were no formal laws governing medical ethics. Egyptian medicine was highly evolved, well regulated by the State, and advanced to a degree that considered it essential, for example, that doctors should specialise in the different branches of clinical medicine and surgery, and of social medicine. There is little, however, that provides evidence of the existence of a code regulating the relationship between patients and doctors. Similarly, other ancient civilisations do not seem to have had codes regulating this relationship. The Mesopotamian Code of Hammurabi (*circa* 1900 BC) seems to come near, however, to specifying the rights of patients and their slaves) in respect of medical (or surgical) torts.[6a, 6b]

It is logical to turn next to Greek medicine, and to Hippocrates, and the works of the Hippocratic corpus, as sources of information on the patient-doctor relationship. The works that are especially relevant, in addition to *Oath*, are *Decorum*, *Law*, *Physician*, and *Precepts*. However, some aspects of the matter are also mentioned in other works, for example *The Art*, *Prognostic*, and *Regimen*.

Nowhere, however, in these and other Hippocratic works, is there any suggestion of a formalised partnership of patient and doctor, or a hint that consent to treatment was to be obtained from the patient in any way, formal or informal. It seems that the fact that the patient had secured the assistance of a physician, and thus had requested his help, was, by implication, a form of consent. But, I must stress, we are not sure that in ancient times the doctor would necessarily feel that this was the case – namely, that consent was necessary, even if only by implication, though clearly a physician might dislike it if his instructions were not followed; and thus, in a way, he expected a consenting patient, a partner in treatment.

I shall try to illustrate these points by quoting from the first two volumes of W H S Jones's translations of the works of Hippocrates.[19, 20]

The need for trust, for example, is revealed in the following passages: '. . . so that men will confidently entrust themselves to him for treatment'.[20a] 'The intimacy between physician and patient is close. Patients in fact put themselves into the hands of their physician . . . So towards all these self-control must be used.'[20b]

This second passage shows the corresponding duty of the physician with regard to his privileged position of trust. Of course, trust is not to be blind, and certainly not indiscriminate, because the physician must be credited with having acquired special knowledge and medical skill: '. . . one is to acquire that ready and infallible habit which we call "the art of medicine". For to do so will bestow a very great advantage upon sick folk and medical practitioners'.[19a] To achieve this aim, 'The course I recommend is to pay attention to the whole of the medical art. Indeed all acts that are good or correct should be in all cases well or correctly performed; if they ought to be done quickly, they should be done quickly, if neatly, neatly, if painlessly, they should be managed with the minimum of pain; and all such acts ought to be performed excellently, in a manner better than that of one's own fellows.'[20c] Basically, the principle guiding the physician in his approach to patients is to strive for excellence, motivated by a desire to serve, as is revealed in the famous sentence '. . for where there is love of man (Φιλανθρωπίη) there is also love of the art'.[19b] This is part of a passage which also considers that it is proper to render services free, but that care of 'the sick to make them well', and of 'the healthy, to keep them well', is not to be divorced from 'care for one's own self', to be 'seemly'.[19b]

Perhaps the following few words from another passage may be construed to indicate that some form of discourse existed between doctor and patient: '. . . care, replies to objections, calm self-control to meet the troubles . . .'.[20d] But it seems equally clear that details of planned treatment (let alone alternatives) were not discussed with the patient: '. . . concealing most things from the patient . . . turning his attention away from what is being done to him; sometimes reprove sharply and emphatically, and sometimes comfort with solicitude and attention, revealing nothing of the patient's future or present condition.'[20e] What matters is that whatsoever is prescribed by the doctor be obeyed by the patient: 'It amounts to this: while physicians may give wrong instructions, patients can never disobey orders. And yet it is much more likely that the sick cannot follow out the orders than that the physicians give wrong instructions. The physician sets about his task with healthy mind and healthy body, having considered the case and past cases of like characteristics to the present, so as to say how they were treated and cured. The patient knows neither what he is suffering from, nor the cause thereof; neither what will be the outcome of his present state, nor the usual results of like conditions. In this state he receives orders, suffering in the present and fearful of the future . . . Which is the more likely: that men in this condition obey, instead of varying, the physician's orders, or that the physician, in the condition that my account has explained above, gives improper orders? Surely it is much more likely that the physician gives proper orders, which the patient not unnaturally is unable to follow . . .'[20f]

As for the most famous of all the works of the Hippocratic corpus, the *Oath* itself, the basic code of Western medical practice, there is nothing in it bearing on consent. It gives guidelines on professional conduct towards patients and towards colleagues. It emphasises respect for teachers, stresses that treatment must be directed towards the patient's benefit, and must avoid harming him, and specifically states that the doctor must not take advantage of his privileged position, must guard professional secrecy, and must not divulge what he learns about people or indulge in gossip. The need to avoid harm, ωφελεῖν ἤ μὴ βλάπτειν,[19c], is an important theme in Hippocratic writings. [The Latin version, *primum* (or *saltem*) *non nocere*, is a rendering from Galen.][21]

It must be upon this type of attitude, injunction to do good and avoid harm, that, especially, the foundation of implicit trust in the doctor lay. Consequently, as already stated, asking for help from the doctor implied that he acted for the patient's good and to the sufferer's advantage, and thus that there was tacit consent.

With regard to the Hippocratic tradition in Alexandria, Greek medical thinking was used as a set of general guidelines, but in essence Alexandrian medicine was based on facts, and on the observation of the sick and dead, rather than on theoretical dogma. Thus a great deal that was new was introduced into medicine: both a general 'philosophy' in the approach to medical science, and anatomy, physiology and morbid anatomy were established. Later, observation was neglected, and the Dogmatists, believers in the written word, appeared on the scene. At the same time, there also arose the Empirics, the antithesis of this school of thought, who believed only in what they could see and observe. They were Hippocratic, nevertheless, but only in the sense that they accepted the basic tenets of medicine formulated by Hippocrates, modifying them in the light of the results of observation. At any rate, the Hippocratic tradition permeated all medical thought, and this led the Alexandrian School of Logical Medicine to collect and catalogue the works attributable to the Coan, to write commentaries on them, and to promote their divulgation. However, as in the case of Roman medicine, little attention seems to have been paid to ethical matters.[6c]

Turning to Roman times, Aulus Cornelius Celsus, who wrote on medicine during the reign of Tiberius, between AD 25 and 35, dealt with the subject according to the three main methods of treating disease – by diet, by drugs and by surgery. In his views on diseases and on their treatment, he followed Hippocrates. Probably the greatest human biologist of antiquity, he subscribed to the ethical principles of Hippocrates,[6d] but it seems that the Oath was not mentioned by him in any of his writings. One should also note the current of pagan humanistic values which, attached to medicine in Greece, percolated into Roman civilisation at this time, albeit for a brief period. Witness especially Scribonius Largus (1st Century AD), and the impassioned words of Libanius.*

In general, however, in Roman times little attention, if any, was paid to ethical aspects of medical work, though the etiquette of medicine received comment. This is certainly

* 'You desired to be one of the healers . . . Now, practice your art faithfully . . . cultivate love of man; if you are called to your patient, hasten to go . . . apply all your mental ability to the case at hand; share in the pain of those who suffer . . . consider yourself a partner in the disease; muster all you know . . . be of your contemporaries the brother, of . . . your elders the son, of those who are younger the father . . . if anyone . . . neglects his own affairs . . . this is not permissible for yourself . . . it is your duty to be to the sick what the Dioscuri are to the sailor (in distress).' Libanius, quoted byEdelstein.[10]

true of Galen (AD 138–201). Of some hundred texts attributed to him, there are some seventeen commentaries on texts of the Hippocratic corpus[40], though a few are lost. It is held that Galen's interpretation of what constituted Hippocratic science and tradition was really a reflection of his own system, albeit with a Hippocratic patina. It is significant that in his works he makes no allusion to *Oath*, and that he has written no commentaries on the other ethical writings of Hippocrates.

THE MIDDLE AGES

The period of the early Middle Ages (the Dark Ages), before the famous Salernitan School established its tradition in medicine, spans about seven hundred years, from about AD 400, say, to about AD 1100. These seven centuries look, in reality, at two very different areas of medical development – Western civilisation, on the one hand, and the Arabic World, on the other.

As far as Western societies are concerned, in the pre-Salernitan era much that was fundamental in the Hippocratic tradition was preserved. MacKinney, an excellent source on this epoch, comments that there was 'much more borrowing from Hippocrates than from Biblical or clerical authorities', but clearly there is also evidence of 'fusion of classical antiquity with Christianity'.[28] The often quoted letter of St Jerome to the priest Nepotian, which is discussed by MacKinney, is a clear demonstration of the persistence in this epoch of the moral aspects of the Coan tradition: 'let it therefore be your duty to keep your tongue chaste as well as your eyes . . . Hippocrates, before he will instruct his pupils, makes them take an oath and compels them to swear obedience to him. That oath exacts from them silence, and prescribes for them their language, gait, dress and manners. How much greater an obligation is laid on us . . .'[28]

The Visigothic code of practice, in Spain, may seem *prima facie* to suggest a form of behaviour with considerable ethical content but, clearly, as the presence of witnesses is required solely because the patient to be bled is a woman, the roomful of witnesses is there to safeguard the doctor against scandal, rather than to support the patient in her hour of need. The Ostrogoths, in Italy, established under Cassiodorus (*circa* AD 550) tight governmental control over the medical profession. In this culture, the patient seems to have been encouraged to question the physician, or at least to ask questions of him: 'let the patient ask you about his ailment, and hear from you the truth about it . . . To make things easier, do not tell the clamoring inquirer what these symptoms signify . . .'.[28] It was expected of the doctor that he should be mindful of the Hippocratic Oath throughout all his work, and indeed, he was required to take an oath. We can discern in this, as well as in the region of Italy where this was a requirement, the beginnings of the Salernitan influence.

If we now turn to Arabic medicine, we note that the Hippocratic tradition persisted when medical knowledge and practice shifted to the Arabic World, but there were no major new contributions to the ethics of medicine, in spite of progress in its practical and more scientific aspects.* Perhaps the greatest figure of Arabic medicine was Avicenna (*circa* AD 1000), and his learned contribution was the *Canon of Medicine*, but it does not appear that he was particularly concerned with the ethical aspects of the profession. Nevertheless, ethics had a say. To Isaac Judaeus (the Elder) is attributed *The Guide of Physicians*, essentially a code of medical conduct.[6e] A celebrated figure of the later period of Arabic medicine is Maimonides (*circa* AD 1100); to him is attributed a prayer in which the physician seeks guidance to save his fellow beings by the use of experience and the application of knowledge: '. . . a cause great and noble is the quest for scientific knowledge whose aim it is to preserve health and life of all creatures. Let my patients lay their trust

* I have deliberately used the expression 'Arabic World' here, to indicate the cultural sphere, rather than 'Islamic' or 'Arab', which imply the religious and ethnic groups, respectively. Either of these terms, construed correctly, would exclude such great figures of Arabic medicine as Maimonides, Isaac Judaeus and Avicenna.

in me and my art, and may they follow my advice and accept my administrations' (translated from Portes[34]). *

A few words should be said on consent in the Jewish tradition. The matter is discussed by Jakobovits in relation to surgery, especially, and to clinical studies and 'experiments' on man.[18] He puts forward tentative guidelines and considerations on the topic of experimental studies on man and on consent, based on the principle that the obligation to preserve life and health is absolute, but also on the premise that some experiments are needed. Interestingly, an important issue appears to be related to consent (or to the absence of a need for it) in relation to necropsy; on this issue Jewish feelings would seem to be particularly strong.

Returning to Western societies, in the late Middle Ages one of the most remarkable steps in the regulation and practical application of medical art and science was taken in the 'Two Sicilies', specifically in Salerno. Although the School in Salerno seems to have been in existence since before the end of the first millenium of the Christian era, the edicts governing the School, medical training, examination, licence to practice and medical conduct stem from legislation dating from the early years of the twelfth century. There are certain important basic changes that occurred in Salerno, perhaps of no direct relevance to the ethical issues discussed here, but nevertheless apposite if medical ethics, as a force capable of moulding action, is not to be considered devoid of meaning and divorced from the reality of matters medical. The Salernitan doctor must have three years of preliminary study in logic, must spend three years of study in medical school (where the approved textbooks are those of Hippocrates and Galen), and must follow this with one year of apprenticeship. A would-be surgeon must also make a special study of anatomy. In 'consideration of the serious

* This attribution is apocryphal. Etziony states that it was first quoted by Markus Herz (*Deutsches Museum*, January 1783). Herz claimed that it was composed by a famous Jewish physician in 12th century Egypt, but in fact he himself was the author, and the Hebrew 'original' was a translation of his alleged 'translation', according to Etziony.[12]

damage and irreparable suffering which may occur as a consequence of the inexperience of physicians, we decree that in future no one who claims the title of physician shall exercise the art of healing or dare to treat the ailing, except such as have beforehand, in our University of Salerno, passed a public examination under a regular teacher of medicine, and have been given a certificate not only by the Professor of Medicine, but also by one of our civil officials, which declares his trustworthiness and sufficient knowledge. This document must be presented to us . . . [Frederick II] . . . and must be followed by the obtaining of a licence to practice medicine . . . Violation of this law is to be punished by confiscation of goods and a year in prison for all those who in future dare to practice medicine without such permission from our authority . . . Every physician given a licence to practice must take an oath that he shall faithfully fulfil all the requirements of the law . . .'.[43]

We can only presume that these legal requirements were matched by moral duties, based on the principles of the Hippocratic tradition. There is good evidence that the elements of the Hippocratic Oath were incorporated in the oath taken at Salerno, the *Civitas Hippocratica*.[4] Other ethical influences, too, were discernible, and might have been derived from the Arab World (for example, Isaac Judaeus the Elder), and medical morality might have been guarded by the *Collegium Doctorum* that was later established in Salerno. Philosophy in Salerno, the *Civitas Aristotelica*, would also have been a source of guidance on ethics in medicine.[26]

At the time of Salerno and later, the ideas on the training of physicians so clearly expounded for that state were also used by the many budding universities and faculties of medicine in Europe. With their development was coupled the preservation of the Hippocratic tracts, mostly the clinical ones. *Aphorisms*, of course, was a favourite, so much so that it qualified for the appellation 'the Physicians' Bible'. *Oath* and the *Lex Hippocratica* (*Law*) were held in high esteem, and were extensively translated and printed (for example in the editions of 'Articella'[24]), or circulated as manuscripts. However, little can be said specifically on ethics, and nothing on consent.

If we disregard the few moral injunctions of the Hippocratic Oath, the preoccupation, reflected in medieval writings on the patient-doctor relationship, with the formalities of etiquette, rather than with the substance of ethics, may seem strange. It could be taken to assume a low regard by the doctors for their moral duties to their patients. However, it must not be forgotten that until there were laws that stipulated training and qualifications (such as the degree course of the Salernitan School, and the State licensing laws in Salerno), and Guilds or Associations, to which doctors belonged, there was no protection against quackery for doctor and patient alike. It is clear from what we read that in antiquity (but also in much more modern times) quackery was practised extensively. It seems probable that quacks were loud, boastful and pompous, given to self-advertising and self-aggrandisement. It must be clear that contrasting behaviour, a demeanour of quiet efficiency and modesty, could be taken to denote a learned man with informed knowledge, and thus a trustworthy person. So etiquette could have been an important distinguishing hallmark of the true and dedicated physician.

MODERN TIMES

We have seen that, so far, questions of *consent* had not entered into the relationship of doctor and patient. Probably more generally, issues relating to *formal* consent had not been raised in either practical (political) social relationships, or in moral attitudes and philosophical thinking. Thus, on the threshold between the Middle Ages and modern times, which will bring 'new formulas' to the fore to guide society, it is appropriate to consider those changes that might have influenced more generally the awareness of subjects with regard to their duties and their rights and introduced the notion of consent, in some form or another – direct or indirect – into matters that governed their daily life.

Not unnaturally, we look at the scene in England, where,

in the face of privileges, the concepts of freedom and of individual rights were soon to emerge, gain 'public support', and become firmly established as traditions in the fabric of society and the ethos of its thinkers. As we approach the end of the Middle Ages, we can perceive not only the gradual shifting of attitudes towards rights tempered with duties, but also the emergence of a spirit of examination of the practical issues and the theory of the (written or unwritten) rules governing interactions between individuals.

In the nature of things, a new 'code' to guide the patient-doctor relationship would have been unlikely to arise until, first, more general rules of conduct between persons had become prevalent, sanctioned by use, and deposited in philosophy, and, secondly, until the profession had set about regulating itself and establishing new codes of conduct, practice and relationships, spelling out on the one hand the extent of privileges, and on the other their boundaries. Consent became part of human interactions, and it seems to have established itself, in practice, as a political reality before it became a philosophical belief. In England it was hammered out when the barons, the knights of the shire and the burgesses in medieval parliaments asserted their corporate right to grant or withhold subsidies to the king, thus continuing within the fused 'houses' the tradition of one of the two (or three) institutions of government, the *Magnum Consilium*. In parallel, the clergy insisted on taxing themselves rather than allowing the crown or parliament to tax them, a pattern that lasted until after the Restoration. Whenever the king summoned the parliament to request a subsidy he sent his mandate to the two archbishops to summon their respective provincial convocations; . . 'and the king would send a member of his council to persuade the Convocation of Canterbury *blandino sermone* to grant an equivalent sum from ecclesiastical revenues. Part of the contest between the Stuart monarchs and parliament was their attempt to raise revenue arbitrarily by means which bypassed consent of the Lords and the Commons in parliament.'[9]

Early in the fifteenth century the physicians themselves

had sought to regularise their position, in anticipation of regulating the profession. Stressing their position in society, by putting 'Fisyk' on the same level as 'Divinitie and Lawe', they petitioned the King, in 1421, to see that the position of doctors be protected and that the proper status be granted to qualified practitioners with a university degree, and that such status be recognised and enforced.[8]

Turning to medical ethics at the beginning of modern times, Larkey discusses the position of Hippocrates and his influence, and especially that of the Oath, in sixteenth-century Elizabethan England.[27] There were many versions of the Oath, but the writings of John Securis have been taken to suggest that it was used almost in a legal sense. He actually discusses the Oath in detail in his book *A Detection and Querimonie of the Daily Enormities and Abuses Committed in Physick*, published in London in 1556 (Larkey[27]) with the aim of exposing defects and promoting improvement in the practice and morality of medicine. It was clear that there was a need, as Securis saw it, to do something about the faults of physicians, and about their privileged position, so that 'some occasion may be geven to refourme the enormities and abuses in the science of Phisicke. And here let no man think that I meane to speake any thing in any point against the privileges and liberties graunted by an act of Parliament to the company or corporation of the Phisitions of London, for I mynde not, nor may not medle with their privileges'.[27]

We are thus coming to times where many radical changes were to be introduced into the formula that had governed the patient-doctor relationship until then. Originally based on the moral precepts which the Greek Hippocratic tradition had set out, and modified – though not radically – by the spirit of Christianity, a new ethical system was evolving which still underlies, basically, the interaction between the patient and his doctor. The beginnings of change, so clearly recognisable in England, as we shall see, started in the seventeenth century, and coincided with the beginning of the scientific revolution and the quest for immutable laws of nature, of man, and in philosophy.

In the wake of the *Statuta Medica* of the (Royal) College of

Physicians, established in 1518, of John Locke's *De Arte Medica** of 1669, and following the publication of John Gregory's *Lectures on the Duties and Qualifications of a Physician*[13], Thomas Percival published, in 1803, his famous book on medical ethics.[33] He was the first, it seems, to use this term. His object was to examine the duties and rules of conduct of doctors: 'The relation in which the physician stands to his patients, to his brethren and to the public are complicated and multifarious: involving much knowledge of human nature and extensive moral duties.' Many are the recommendations on morality and behaviour in the many situations (hospital and private practice, the law, and so on) in which the doctor may find himself. Two points made by Percival are especially worth noting. The first concerns experimental treatments in medicine and surgery, which, he states, are not to be undertaken without a proper consultation between all concerned, and only in accordance with sound reasons. Secondly, Percival stresses 'let both the physician and the surgeon never forget that their professions** are public trusts . . .'.[33]

By then the College of Physicians had been established for over 250 years, and the first attempt at medical legislation by the sovereign was almost 400 years old; barbers and surgeons, until then joined by the second Medical Act of 1540, had just dissolved the United Company. In 1815 the Apothecaries Act established the first statutory insistence upon apprenticeship, examination and licensing; and the very success of the Act led to further developments. The Medical Reform Movement produced at Worcester in 1832 the Provincial Medical and Surgical Association, which became in 1855 the British Medical Association; and then the Medical Act of 1858 which established the General Council of Medical Education and Registration, now the General Medical Council. It was given quasi-judicial powers over the profession, as a body set up to safeguard the public interest, and to

* Quoted by Jonsen.[22]

** *Professio* was first applied to medicine by Scribonius, in the same sense that we would use the word 'vocation'.[10]

promote an enviable, and envied, standard of ethics for the profession in its daily affairs.[35] In 1847, the American Medical Association had published its first code of medical ethics.[1] In introducing this on behalf of the Ethics Committee, Dr I Hays acknowledged its straight descent from Percival's principles of medical ethics, even to the extent of almost *verbatim* quotations from the book. Though there were a number of revisions, it was not until 110 years after its first publication that the code was more radically revised – and even then only to remove 'prolixity and ambiguity'.

I can summarise my notes so far by suggesting that until the turn of the century, or – more likely – the end of the First World War, the patient-doctor relationship was guided by a standard of ethics that was based on trust and confidence on the one hand, and a spirit of dedication and what has been called *noblesse oblige* on the other. This was backed by the requirement of appropriate training, first in the form of simple apprenticeship as in the Greek *polis*, then by the institution of more formal teaching, and the establishment of universities and faculties of medicine in line with the pattern set by Salerno under Frederick II. The example of the Salernitan School of Medicine was followed by Bologna, Montpellier, Vienna, Basel, and all other European universities. With the establishment of medical faculties, the prescribing of lectures, the recommendation of textbooks and the specifying of the duration of courses, there followed graduation, licensing, and taking of oaths of allegiance to professional standards. Later, professional guilds and associations were set up, often charged also with determining ethical codes. In addition, in Western societies, already from the late Middle Ages (and in some civilisations even before), the profession was disciplined, and its principles were regulated, by the sovereign, or the state and government through the power delegated by society. In some societies, the profession itself set up its ethical watchdog, armed with judicial teeth, as in Great Britain. In a sense, the idea of physicians regulating other physicians was not new: the concept harks back to the essence of the Hippocratic

Oath. Nevertheless, along with all these regulations and, fundamentally, at the levels of person to person, the patient-doctor relationship was guided by the laws of trust and by duties, tinged with a mixture of autonomy, authority and paternalism.

Changes in society, science and medicine: the origin of formal consent

Soon after this period of increasing control over what was nevertheless an essentially personal code of professional morality – and certainly between the two World Wars – the formula of the relationship altered. We realise now that there had occurred a number of changes, in the profession and in patients, as people, which underlay the modified relationship and called for codes, and regulations and clarifications of rights, as well as of duties.

One of the questions is: what were these changes? A second is: what were the changes in society, and in the way man considered himself, which led, in parallel, to a change of attitude to medicine? And, a third: by what formal mechanisms did these changed attitudes alter the patient-doctor relationship? Let me start by looking at the first question, namely, what the changes were. Since the end of the First World War, and with a continuing crescendo, medical knowledge based on scientific facts has increased at a rate faster than at any previous time in history. Perhaps it is not out of place to recall that more than 80 per cent of all the scientists that ever lived are still alive today. The changes in medical knowledge, ranging from treatment to prevention, from diagnosis to prognosis, from laboratory practice to bedside monitoring, have affected the doctor, his skills, the way in which he is taught, his continuing education, and indeed even his ability to understand technical progress and its implications for and applications to the handling of patients. However, the changes have also affected the patients themselves, the public, who have become accustomed not only to consider that science is 'the art of the soluble', but also to expect that the application of scientific knowledge to the treatment of disease is actually an 'art of the possible'.* The public now expects, therefore, success in treatment; in other words, the patient expects to be cured. Cure, one suspects, is almost automatically taken for granted. Consequently, failure to cure is attributed to ignorance, which may amount to negligence, and – at best – is alleged to be the result of lack of due care and attention. I am led to wonder how much the imperceptible shift from *is* to *ought*[16] (that is, the confusion between *is* and *ought*[31]), cloaks issues centering on the change in absolute expectation from *curare* to *sanare*,** a change which has undoubtedly been fuelled by the ever-increasing and widespread communication of ideas and opinions among many potential patients. Certainly, the fusion of the new methodology of science with the traditionally observational art of medicine has made medical praxis more complex and difficult. It has increased the need for specialisation, and this has often broken up the unity of medical responsibility for the patient and the one-to-one relationship between physician and sufferer. The aging population in Western societies has meant that people are likely to suffer from multiple ills and may often require handling by different specialists, with a further splintering of the one-to-one relationship. In addition, investigative medicine has introduced the non-medical scientist as part of the medical team, with the effect of adding to the involvement of the medical man with the scientific effort. Add to this the physician's realisation of the many uncertainties that surround the practice of medicine, the knowledge of sickness and health, the effects of drugs, and so on; and medicine, it was recognised, was much more experimental than had been thought to be the case. Observation alone was inadequate, and much more experimental and enquiring approaches were needed: 'In the philosophic sense, observation shows, and experiment teaches'.[3a] Ultimately, it was felt that only man could offer

* Paraphrased from the review of Arthur Koestler's *The Act of Creation*, quoted in *The Art of the Soluble*.[30]

** *Curare*: to care for, treat; *sanare*: to heal, restore to health.

the solution – through experiments – to many of the existing human problems in medicine. Indeed, what Claude Bernard had written, a century before, was becoming part of the fabric of modern medicine. 'For we must not deceive ourselves, morals do not forbid making experiments on one's neighbor or on one's self; in everyday life men do nothing but experiment on one another. Christian morals forbid only one thing, doing ill to one's neighbor. So, among the experiments that may be tried on man, those that can only do harm are forbidden, those that are innocent are permissible, and those that may do good are obligatory'.[3b] A good example of what was happening, where a solution by experiment on man was needed, is offered by the streptomycin trial for the treatment of pulmonary tuberculosis[41,15] (see also Chapter 7 by Philipp and Johnson, *infra*).* As a result of these changes in modern medicine, the doctor tends now to reflect a less homely professional image than in the past, and his patients sometimes seem to perceive his allegiances less clearly than they used to.

Before turning to my third question – concerning the formal mechanics whereby the changes already discussed resulted in a modification of the patient-doctor relationship – I should consider again (see p 67) the societal setting and the altered attitudes that must also have been responsible for the changes that occurred with regard to attitudes to medicine, by describing the background against which these changes occurred. Clearly they must have been related to, and impelled by, the rise of philosophical liberalism during the period between the middle of the seventeenth century and the middle of the eighteenth. Two *leitmotifs* are characteristic of this movement: that the capacity for free decision is a hallmark of man, and that the right to express and, indeed, to set about exercising this capacity is one of the key 'human rights'. Expressions of these attitudes and feelings are to be found in the attempt to clarify and define those

* It should be noted that this trial, cited as a model for all modern therapeutic trials, was actually conducted in 1946 *without* patient consent.

human rights that were the property of all men, so that boundaries might be erected to contain the exercise of political, and social, power. Life and liberty were certainly considered to be the principal human rights. On the philosophical side, Locke, writing in the 1680s, and Kant (*circa* 1780) may be cited among the main exponents of the belief in the Rights of Man. On the political side, we have Bills of Rights – in other words, curbs on the use of political and executive power, and guidelines for its exercise.[39] These rights were explicitly stated in the famous words of the American Declaration of Independence, on 4 July 1776: '. . . to secure these rights, governments are instituted among men, deriving their just powers from the consent of the governed'; we should note that the key word here is 'consent'. These sentiments were echoed by the French Declaration of the Rights of Man, in 1789, which referred to man's 'Natural and Imprescriptible' rights. Perhaps one may be allowed to think that the word 'natural' here relates to the doctrine of natural law (see, for example, the works of St Thomas Aquinas). To this doctrine, and to Kantian deontology, one can add what may perhaps be considered the third pillar of ethical theory – utilitarianism. This is based especially on the thinking and the works of John Stuart Mill (*circa* 1850), and aims at producing, as a consequence of action, the greatest balance of good over evil, while considering every person involved. Mill thought that the intrinsic value of utilitarianism lay in the principle of maximum happiness.

It is against this ferment of philosophical and political ideas that the concept of patient consent has evolved and matured in medicine, almost naturally. Consent – 'informed consent' – is taken to serve the ethical function of promoting individual autonomy[5], and autonomy has a position of central importance in biomedical ethics.

All this is part of the background that has recently led to the extensive discussion of the ethics, responsibilities, and practice of investigations on human subjects, and to writings and deliberations on these topics. See, for example, the Medical Research Council statement on Responsibility in

Investigations on Human Subjects[11,37], the Code of Ethics of the World Medical Association, known as the Declaration of Helsinki (see *Dictionary of Medical Ethics*[7] and Appendix B), the Report of the Royal College of Physicians Committee on the Supervision of the Ethics of Clinical Research Investigations in Institutions[38], and the British Paediatric Association's Guidelines to Aid Ethical Committees Considering Research Involving Children[14]. One notes that in these guidelines and declarations, a clear distinction is made between 'clinical research combined with professional care' and 'non-therapeutic research'.

This brings me to the question which I raised; namely, that which concerns the *mechanisms* or *ways* whereby the patient-doctor relationship was altered. With regard to this, and in line with the distinction between therapeutic and non-therapeutic research, Beauchamp and Childress[2] make an important point when they consider the mode of origin of informed consent in medicine. They believe that consent can be traced 'historically to two sources: (1) standards for medical *practice* have derived from case law, and (2) standards for *research* have grown from their roots in both the Nuremberg Code, and the Declaration of Helsinki'. These, then, can be considered the two mechanisms which, through the need for formal informed consent, introduced a profound change in the relationship between patient and physician.

Considering case law first, perhaps the beginnings of the practice on consent may be traced to a declaration in an Illinois appellate court in 1905/1906: '. . . the free citizen's first and greatest right . . . – the right to the inviolability of his person, in other words, his right to himself – is the subject of universal acquiescence, and this right necessarily forbids a physician or surgeon . . . to violate without permission the bodily integrity of his patient . . .'.[5] The need for informed consent is said to have been 'feebly called' in 1957 by the American judge Justice Bray*, but to have been strongly

* *Salgo v Leland Stanford, Jr University Board of Trustees.* 317 P 2d 170, 181.

supported in 1960 by Justice Schroeder.* The following statement pertains to this case: 'Anglo-American law starts with the premise of thorough-going self-determination. It follows that each man is considered to be master of his own body . . .' (quoted by Katz[23]).

I have already introduced the question of the origin of the Nuremberg Code on p58 (see also Appendix A), and clearly the issue of 'human experimentation' has become a formidable one in the wake of the inhuman atrocities in Germany and its occupied and allied territories around the time of the Second World War, an awful chapter which is only now drawing to a close. Unfortunately, it must be realised that it is highly unlikely that laws of ethics, codes and declarations can, *per se*, constitute a safeguard against, or a deterrent to, the type of utterly criminal behaviour witnessed at that time. Conversely, however, codes and declarations are fundamental to the situation considered in these notes.

In a discussion on informed consent, it is insufficient to offer definitions of meaning, as was done in the opening sentences of this paper. A procedural description is needed – namely, a description of what is involved in the practice of informed consent. The American Department of Health, Education and Welfare gives the following criteria:

'"Informed consent" means the knowing consent of an individual or his legally authorised representative, so situated as to be able to exercise free power of choice without undue inducement or any element of force, fraud, deceit, duress, or other form of constraint or coercion. The basic elements of information necessary to such consent include:

1 A fair explanation of the procedures to be followed, and their purposes, including identification of any procedures which are experimental;
2 A description of any attendant discomforts and risks reasonably to be expected;
3 A description of any benefits reasonably to be expected;
4 A disclosure of any appropriate alternative procedures that might be advantageous for the subject;

* *Natanson v Kline*. 350 P 2d 1093 (1960) and 354 P 2d 670 (1960).

5 An offer to answer any queries concerning the procedures;
6 An instruction that the person is free to withdraw his consent and to discontinue participation in the project or activity at any time without prejudice to the subject.'[42]

It is important to make two further points about the subject of informed consent. First, truly informed consent implies *complete* patient-doctor participation, and rests on what Ramsey defines as the 'cardinal canon of loyalty joining men together in medical practice and investigation'.[36] The second point is related to the validity, as well as the essence, of informed consent. Ingelfinger[17], who is concerned with the procedural, applied side of informed consent, doubts whether most persons are able to understand fully, or even just adequately, the information imparted to them by physician/investigators. He also believes that there is a risk of 'overwhelming' the patient/subject with information which may amount to a subtle form of coercion. The consequences of this, and, in any case, the failure to understand at least adequately, may lead to 'informed consent' becoming in practice 'informed but uneducated consent'. A similar point is made by Judge Spotswood W Robinson III in *Canterbury v Spence* (already discussed).[29]

Conclusions

I have attempted to review the origin of 'patient consent' in medicine, an integral part of the patient-doctor relationship. Indissolubly bound to both the concept and the practice of consent is 'informed consent'.

It is customary to consider informed consent *vis à vis* two sets of medical activities: treatment and research. The latter, sometimes known as human experimentation, includes – for example – the conduct of clinical trials, the assessment of drugs in treatment, the placebo and double-blind research designs, the use of volunteers, proxy consent, research on children, research on fetuses, and so on. Treatment, too, has wide boundaries, and includes surgery, prophylaxis, prenatal diagnosis, transplantation, and other hotly debated issues, such as proxy permission for treatment, competence to decide, and so on. Both activities are sensitive to the issue of whether consent is (ever) truly informed (rather than just adequate or even 'uneducated'), and to the issue of proxy consent and many others, and it is clear that the distinction between treatment and research is often blurred.

It is widely held that the *formal* application of the principles which specified the need for 'informed consent' originated separately, by two distinct, convergent routes. Informed consent with regard to *treatment* is considered to be a derivative of the application of case law to clinical matters, and to have become established, probably, around the late 1950s. In contrast, it is thought that attention was focused on *research* on man especially by what transpired at the Nuremberg Trials, and after the declaration of the Nuremberg Code in 1947.[32]

However, these must have been, in a sense, only the formal expressions of principles that had become ingrained in the structure of society, and of medicine. The fundamental principles on which the practice of consent rests must have evolved gradually from the wide appreciation in the community of a basic set of ideas concerning the individual person; ideas which have been gradually guiding the development of Western societies, regulating the interaction between individuals and moulding the way in which they were governing themselves. Many would feel that the basic tenet on which the need for consent is built is the principle of autonomy. Other principles which must be considered along with autonomy, and which are relevant especially to the patient-doctor relationship, are paternalism and authority. These principles, which underlie informed consent, are considered key issues in biomedical ethics.

It is clear that the practice (namely the application) of informed consent has had a beneficial effect in concentrating attention on how to achieve 'informed consent', that is on the need to impart information. It is implicit in the formula 'informed consent' that the patient has been given information and that, consequently, he is 'informed'; this, in turn, implies that he has understood the information, and that his consent – if given – is a 'knowing consent' (see p 77). On the positive side, striving for informed consent means that the doctor attempts to explain by attuning himself to his lay patient, that is, to the level of his understanding. And this is not only essential for the patient but may, at times, turn out to be salutary for the doctor. On the negative side, the practice of consent, and its relation, in part, to litigation, can almost cause the doctor to go to the other extreme, that of over-investigation (to be 'on the safe side'; as a 'double check'), and this in turn introduces the real possibility of additional risks to the patient (see Chapter 7 by Philipp and Johnson).

In a discussion on the origin of consent, it is appropriate to consider briefly the 'stability' of the present situation, because – if not stable, and thus transitory – the causes of its instability, and especially the consequences, are important. My feeling is that the present position is in a state of unstable equilibrium. I am unable to perceive, however, the direction in which this balance will shift. In a sense, as I have been wont to say, the relationship between patient and doctor is based not on contract, but on covenant, by which I mean that it is not a relationship based on law or business, but an interaction which binds individuals through morality. To find ways of strengthening this relationship without having recourse to the law is perhaps the main task in the practice and art of modern scientific medicine.

Summary

Consent was not considered part of the formal (or informal) patient-doctor relationship in antiquity and the Middle Ages. For a long time – perhaps almost twenty centuries – the ethics and etiquette of the Hippocratic tradition guided this relationship. During this time the medical profession was gradually evolving from a clannish apprenticeship to the establishment of formal training and the setting up of university courses and faculties of medicine. Meanwhile, doctors were organising themselves into professional guilds, and, later, into associations, and these in due course established guidelines on ethical matters relating to the practice of medicine. They were also charged with exercising disciplinary control over medical conduct. Defence societies were also a novel but late development. However, the issue of consent was apparently not considered until recent times. For example, the standard work on medical ethics, by Thomas Percival[33], dating from the start of the nineteenth century, makes no mention of it. Thus, until the end of the First World War, the relationship between patients and doctors remained based on trust, on the one hand, and on a sense of duty and devotion on the other. The increasing complexity of medicine, and its increasing technological and scientific input, was certainly a circumstantial factor which – coupled with changes in the public's expectations of medicine – gradually led to a change in the rules of the relationship. This change can be seen to have a formal expression in the practice of 'informed consent'. It is considered to rest on the enunciation of important philosophical principles, and on radical changes of attitude to the 'human rights' issues. This was a factor in the setting of limits to political and social power. Consent itself is seen to have received its formal derivations from case law, impinging upon the practice of medicine, and from codes attempting to regulate professional conduct and human experimentation.

References

1 American Medical Association. Code of medical ethics. *Proceedings of the National Medical Convention* 1846–1847. pp 83–106.

2 Beauchamp, T L and Childress, J F. *Principles of biomedical ethics.* Oxford, Oxford University Press, 1979. pp 62–63.

3 Bernard, Claude. *An introduction to the study of experimental medicine: translated by* H C Greene, (1865). New York, Dover, 1957.
  a p 5
  b p 102

4 Cantarella, Raffaele. Una tradizione ippocratica nella scuola Salernitana: il giuramento dei medici. *Archeion: archívio di storia della scienza,* vol XV, 1933. pp 305–320.

5 Capron, A M. Informed consent in catastrophic diseases and

treatment. *University of Pennsylvania Law Review*, vol 123. 1974. pp 364–376.

6 Castiglioni, Arturo. *A history of medicine*. [translated from the Italian and edited by E B Krumbhaar]. New York, Jason Aronson, 1975.
   a p 59
   b p 40
   c p 184
   d p 204–212
   e p 272

7 Duncan, A S and others. eds. *Dictionary of medical ethics*. Revised edition. London, Darton, Longman and Todd; New York, Crossroad, 1981. pp 132–135.

8 Dunstan, G R. The doctor-patient relationship. In: Wood, C. ed. *Health and the family*. London, Academic Press; New York, Grune and Stratton, 1979. pp. 185–192.

9 Dunstan, G R. Personal communication. 1981.

10 Edelstein, Ludwig. The professional ethics of the Greek physician. *Bulletin of the History of Medicine*, vol XXX, no 5. September/October, 1956. pp 391–419.

11 Ethics of human experimentation. *British Medical Journal*, vol II, no 5402. 18 July, 1964. pp 135–136.

12 Etziony, M B. *The physician's creed*. Springfield, Illinois, Charles C Thomas, 1973. p 28.

13 Gregory, John. *Lectures on the duties and qualifications of a physician*. London, W Strahan and T Cadell, 1772.

14 Guidelines to aid ethical committees considering research involving children: British Paediatric Association working party on ethics of research in children. *Archives of Disease in Childhood*, vol 55, no 1. January, 1980. pp 75–77.

15 Hill, Sir Austin Bradford. Medical ethics and controlled trials. *British Medical Journal*, vol I, no 5337. 20 April, 1963. pp 1043–1049.

16 Hume, David. *A treatise of human nature* (1739–40). Oxford, Oxford University Press, 1978.

17 Ingelfinger, F J. Informed (but uneducated) consent. *New England Journal of Medicine*, vol 287, no 9. 31 August, 1972. pp 465–466.

18 Jakobovits, Immanuel. *Jewish medical ethics*. New York, Bloch, 1975. pp 279–293.

19 Jones, W H S. [translator] *Hippocrates*, vol I. [English translation from the Greek]. London, Heinemann, 1972.

a *Precepts*, pp 314–315
b *Precepts*, pp 318–319
c *Epidemics*, pp 164–165

20 Jones, W H S. [translator] *Hippocrates*, vol II. [English translation from the Greek]. London, Heinemann, 1967.
a *Prognostic*, pp 6–7
b *Physician*, pp 312–313
c *Regimen in acute diseases*, pp 64–65
d *Decorum, XII*, pp 294–295
e *Decorum, XVI*, pp 296–297, 298–299
f *Art, VII*, pp 200–201, 202–203

21 Jonsen, Albert R. Do no harm: axiom of medical ethics. In: Spicker, Stuart F and Engelhardt, H T. eds. *Philosophical medical ethics: its nature and significance*. Dordrecht, Holland, D Reidel, 1977. pp 27–41.

22 Jonsen, A R. Do no harm. *Annals of Internal Medicine*, vol 88, no 6. June, 1978. pp 827–832.

23 Katz, J. Disclosure and consent: in search of their roots. In: Milunsky, A and Annas, G J. eds. *Genetics and the law II*. New York and London, Plenum Press, 1980. pp 121–130.

24 Kibre, Pearl. Hippocratic writings in the Middle Ages. *Bulletin of the History of Medicine*, vol 18, no 4. November, 1945. pp 371–412.

25 Kieffer, G H. *Bioethics: a textbook of issues*. London, Addison-Wesley, 1979. p 238.

26 Kristeller, Paul O. The School of Salerno: its development and its contribution to the history of learning. *Bulletin of the History of Medicine*, vol 17, no 2. February, 1945. pp 138–194.

27 Larkey, S V. The Hippocratic oath in Elizabethan England. *Bulletin of the History of Medicine*, vol IV, 1936. pp 201–219.

28 MacKinney, Loren C. Medical ethics and etiquette in the early middle ages: the persistence of Hippocratic ideals. *Bulletin of the History of Medicine*, vol XXVI, no 1. January-February, 1952. pp 1–31.

29 Mappes, T and Zembaty, J. *Biomedical ethics*. New York, McGraw Hill, 1980. pp 79–81.

30 Medawar, P B. *The art of the soluble*. London, Methuen, 1967. p 7.

31 Morison, R S. Reflections on some social implications of modern biology. *Zygon*, vol 11, no 2. 1976, pp 96–114.

32 Pappworth, M H. *Human guinea pigs: experimentation on man*. London, Routledge and Kegan Paul, 1967. pp 185–219.

33 Percival, T. (1803) *Medical Ethics. Or, a Guide to Institutions and Precepts Adapted to the Professional Conduct of Physicians and Surgeons.* Manchester: printed by S. Russell, for J. Johnson, St Paul's Churchyard, and R. Bickerstaff, the Strand, London.
34 Portes, L. Preface. In: *Le code de deontologie medicale.* Paris, Conseil National de l'Ordre des Medecins, 1947. pp 31–41.
35 Poynter, F N L. ed. *The evolution of medical practice in Britain.* London, Pitman Medical, 1961.
36 Ramsey, Paul. *The patient as person: explorations in medical ethics.* New Haven, Yale University Press, 1970. pp 266–275.
37 Responsibility in investigations on human subjects: statement by Medical Research Council. *British Medical Journal,* vol II, no 5402. 18 July, 1964. pp 178–180.
38 Royal College of Physicians: *Report of the committee on the supervision of the ethics of clinical research investigations in institutions.* London, Royal College of Physicians, 1973.
39 Scarman, Lord L G C. *Human rights.* [Lecture delivered at the Senate House, University of London, 18 October, 1973. Unpublished.]
40 Smith, Wesley. *The Hippocratic tradition.* New York, Cornell University Press, 1979. pp 61–176.
41 Streptomycin treatment of pulmonary tuberculosis: a Medical Research Council investigation. *British Medical Journal,* vol II, no 4582. 30 October, 1948. pp 769–782.
42 United States. Department of Health, Education and Welfare. *Code of federal regulations, title 45, US Code, part 46.* Revised edition, Washington, DHEW, 1978. p 103C.
43 Walsh, James J. *The Popes and science: the history of the papal relations to science during the middle ages and down to our own time.* New York, Fordham University Press, 1908. pp. 419–421.
44 Wolstenholme, G E W and O'Connor, Maeve. eds. Appendix 1: the Nuremberg code. In: Ciba Foundation. *Ethics in medical progress: with special reference to transplantation.* London, J and A Churchill, 1966.

My thanks are due to Mrs B A Merchant, Research Librarian, Paediatric Research Unit, and Miss H Stadler, Assistant Librarian, for their invaluable assistance in tracing the references, and to my Research Secretary, Miss Elizabeth Manners, for her help with the manuscript.

Appended Note on Consent in Law by Ian Kennedy

Whatever obscurities and ambiguities there may have been in the Hippocratic tradition and professional practice of medicine, it has always been part of the English law that a touching which has not been consented to is a civil wrong and may be a crime. This appears as early as Bracton. In his treatise, *De Legibus Angliae*, written *circa* 1250–58, he mentions the defence of *volenti non fit injuria*, and thereby he implies that in the absence of willingness a crime or civil wrong would be committed. The Year Book in 1305 has a case explaining the need for and effect of consent in the context of trespass to the person.

What is important perhaps is the point at which people began to complain of touchings by doctors which had not been consented to. And, of course, complaints arise only if there is a sense of something being wrong. For the lawyer one has to go beyond complaint, however, and discover when it became part of received wisdom that a complaint could properly take the form of a legal action. The fact that the law forbade something did not, of course, mean that the practice was unknown. Indeed, one's sense is that touchings by doctors without consent were commonplace. To discover the point historically when it was perceived that a legal remedy might exist one has to examine when people became aware of what the law provided. This awareness came much earlier to the literate middle class than to the rest.

But there is still another point which must be weighed historically, namely, the time when professionalism, in this case medical professionalism, became susceptible of challenge; for even knowing that one had a legal right and perhaps a legal remedy may not have been enough if the status of the professional was such as to make it difficult or unlikely that he would be challenged. Thus, the enquiry as to when consent in legal terms became noticeably relevant is not readily answered by reference only to the first case or two. Rather, there was obviously a gradual process, which calls for some knowledge of social history and medical sociology, in which legal principles which had always existed began to be applied and enforced in the context of the doctor and patient. It is a fair guess that, except in outrageous cases in which lack of consent may have been pressed for as long as there have been doctors, the last third of the nineteenth century is the period during which actions appeared in the courts.

The relevance of consent was initially confined to the tort of trespass, particularly battery, in that the argument was that there was no battery, no unconsented touching, since the patient consented. By the 1940s and 1950s in England and the United States of America it was clear that battery was too blunt an instrument to deal with the problem, which was perceived as being a violation of the patient's interest in being free from unwanted physical assault. Battery could be avoided by having the patient consent in general terms. The courts thus began to look to the tort of negligence to protect the patient's interests. Negligence consists of a breach of duty owed to the patient. One of the components of this duty the courts decided was the duty to obtain an informed consent from the patient such that if none was obtained the doctor was negligent. Thus consent took on a new life, which is still very vital, in the form of a requirement of professional duty and consequently a right of every patient, subject to exceptions. The old law of trespass (battery) still exists, but it is comparatively rare to see it alleged, since it has reverted to its status as a wholly unconsented touching.

Consent and minors

The principles governing the giving of consent by proxy on behalf of minors (as of other legally incompetent persons) for a medical intervention designed for their good are fairly clear. There are, however, some more difficult questions: can parents over-rule the consent of a fully understanding and intellectually capable minor, say a child of fourteen years, or can the refusal of consent by such a minor over-rule the wish of parents that, for instance, a surgical operation be performed?

Some propositions may be offered.

1 Clearly the particular facts will be crucial, but there must be certain principles discoverable in law and practice.
2 Reference to practice reminds us that any principle or rule must be one which works and does not offend the sensibilities of society generally or of doctors.
3 There are few if any legal statements on these problems in the form of cases or of statute, though there is case law in America upholding the view that the will of the comprehending minor should prevail in most circumstances, whether it be to give or to withhold consent.
4 Any rule which called for the ignoring by a doctor of a *refusal* of treatment by a comprehending minor may well be objectionable to doctors since they would be dealing with a patient by force ultimately (and this is different from the six-year-old child having his teeth checked or filled over his objections, since we assume that he doesn't know what is best for him).
5 It may be necessary to draw a distinction between treatments which threaten life and/or limb and others, although this may in some circumstances be a bad distinction.
6 This said, it may be suggested:
a) when the comprehending minor *consents*, the consent is valid and the doctor may rely on it. (This, after all, is the legal issue, since legal challenge would come from the parents (or seldom from the child), alleging that the doctor should not have relied on it.) This proposition may be subject to the rider that if the proposed treatment is threatening to life and/or limb, then the consent *may* not be valid. It is suggested that the doctor's best course in such a case, if the parents sought to override the consent, would be to petition the court for a declaration as to the validity of the consent. This could be done very quickly, within a day or two. The proposition is also subject to the rider that certain things may not be consented to by anyone, minor or no, and that minors specifically may not consent to certain things, for example, to tattooing under the Tattooing of Minors Act, 1969.
b) where the comprehending minor *withholds consent*, in circumstances in which the parent has given it, it could be

said that good practice as well as legal doctrine require that the refusal be respected, even if the treatment may be life or limb saving, and *a fortiori* if it be life or limb threatening. Some may not agree with this, but there is authority in the USA.[1]

Reference

1 Veatch, R M. *Death, dying, and the biological revolution: our last quest for responsibility*. New Haven, Yale University Press, 1977.

7

CONSIDERATIONS GOVERNING A DOCTOR'S ADVICE TO HIS PATIENT

Elliot E Philipp and E Stewart Johnson

The doctor-patient relationship

A successful relationship between a patient and his doctor depends on a mutually acceptable agreement. This usually begins with the doctor's willingness or consent to take on the responsibility of caring for the patient, and the patient's agreement or consent to being cared for by the doctor. Three main advantages are intended to result from a patient's consent to treatment. The first is the involvement of the patient in the decisions taken about his illness. The second is that the doctor has the full cooperation of the patient. The third is that the doctor is relieved of some of the burden of responsibility if the agreed treatment fails – an advantage with medico-legal implications for the doctor. The weighting given to each of these factors depends in part on the personalities and characters of both doctor and patient.

Obtaining consent

According to Wilkinson 'In medical and surgical practice . . . consent to examination or treatment must always be obtained, even if the fact that the patient has sought advice implies consent to what is to be done'.[30] He elaborates on the cases of children under 16 years of age, when the written consent of one of the parents must be obtained, and of patients who are unconscious or of unsound mind, when the consent of a near relative should be obtained. Where such consent cannot be obtained, treatment should be confined to the minimum necessary to deal with the emergency.

This chapter attempts to explain the present position of consent in current medical practice as it applies to different circumstances and the inter-relationships between patient and doctor and often a third party, such as an employer, life insurance company or the state.

The mere fact that the patient has entered the doctor's surgery is in itself taken as consent to discuss his illness. But the doctor is not entitled to touch the patient, let alone examine him, without the latter's consent. This need not be given in writing but should be verbally communicated. A suitable phrase that is often used to obtain such consent is 'Would you like me to examine you?' or 'Would you like to get on the couch?'. The touching of a patient without such consent is technically an assault. Were the patient to lie voluntarily on the doctor's examination couch this would be an example of non-verbal consent.

One of the defects of the British National Health Service is that it requires the general practitioner, in particular, to have so many patients on his list that he can allow on average only five or six minutes for each consultation.[15] Hospital doctors in outpatient clinics may be not much better placed. These short meetings may be inadequate for making any but the most obvious diagnoses, unless the doctor knows the patient and his family well. This time factor inevitably influences both the quality and the amount of advice a doctor will give his patient, on the basis of which the patient will consent or not consent to treatment.

It is essential that any information given by the doctor should be within the capacity of the patient to understand. Doctors often do not understand what the patient is driving at, just as the patient may not understand what the doctor intends. For instance, a patient may come complaining of some imaginary or very minor speech defect in her child, when what she really wants to talk about is the child's relationship with his father. The importance of adequate discussion of a patient's problem cannot be overemphasised, but there is a need for this discussion to be controlled carefully by the doctor; otherwise instead of helping the patient, it may prove harmful. The doctor must ensure that no undisciplined discussion takes place.

To the verbal communication which people, including doctors and patients, make towards one another, must be added the non-verbal signals they use intentionally or otherwise. Non-verbal signals make up for something lacking in words, and words make up for what is lacking in expressions and gestures. It is very easy to say something with one's lips while the expression in the eyes fails to support the words uttered.[9]

A doctor has to listen to what the patient is saying with all its nuances before he gives advice. He has to watch for the balance between organic and non-organic disease. He has to overcome, unless he has been skilfully trained, any conscious or unconscious personal inhibitions he may have to listening to subjects that he finds difficult, such as perhaps sex, hatred or suicide. He may resent becoming emotionally involved with his patient. He may fail to appreciate that the patient's ability to communicate has been altered either by illness or by drugs. Above all he may consciously or unconsciously like or dislike his patient irrationally. The doctor, if he is to render a true service to his patients, has to attempt to balance out any bias he may have in any direction.

Thus he may give a service which is different from that which he originally contemplated.

Making diagnoses

Clinical investigations may be invasive or non-invasive. Non-invasive investigations are unlikely to do any harm; possible exceptions are those such as repeated x-ray examinations or x-ray examinations during pregnancy. Invasive investigations, by introducing apparatus or chemicals into the patient, tend to carry greater risks and usually require more formal consent, sometimes in writing.

When reaching the diagnosis of an illness involves procedures that can be painful, upsetting or harmful, or may involve an operation or examination under a general anaesthetic, the patient is, in strict routine, asked for a written consent before any such procedure is carried out. Similarly with all new or experimental procedures such written consent must be requested.

Treatment and its acceptance by the patient

Once the diagnosis has been made, treatment may follow. It is known that some 50 per cent of all those who consent to commence long-term treatment fail to complete the treatment as instructed.[16] This non-compliance results in an unnecessary major cost on the community as well as depriving the patient of the benefits he may derive from the medicine or treatment. There are those who agree to take treatment and do take everything offered, but there are also those who agree but never intend to follow the treatment. Others may refuse to follow advice, and may in this way endanger not only themselves but society as well. It is the duty of someone with an infection to be treated for his own sake and, in order to avoid transmitting it, to have the infection eradicated if it is communicable. So, an infected person may need to take antibiotics not only to cure himself but for the good of society.

In England and Wales individual rights are never regarded as absolutely inviolate although many of the *desiderata* of the European Commission on Human Rights are accepted. The right of a patient to *refuse* treatment may lapse if he is suffering from a serious infection such as diphtheria or lassa fever. A patient with these conditions cannot refuse to be isolated from the community until he is no longer infectious. Similarly a typhoid carrier should be prevented from preparing food because of the grave risk of infecting all who may partake of the meals he prepares.

In the control of sexually transmitted diseases there is a moral duty on the part of both patient and doctor to prevent, by adequate treatment, its spread, but there is no legal obligation for the patient to seek treatment. The law guards a person's civil liberty against overwhelming intrusion by the state.

Choosing treatment

Occasionally the patient has to make a choice between different forms of treatment or prophylaxis such as, for instance, choosing from all the various forms of contraception that are available. It is common experience that where the patient has received ideas on birth control from the media, from relatives and from friends, she will tend to choose the form of treatment on which she has set her mind even before she has seen the doctor rather than such other forms of treatment as the medical practitioner may suggest. It is an imprudent doctor who, if there are no medical contra-indications, presses contraceptive methods other than those which the patient suggests. In the event that he feels that he must, because of the patient's medical condition, he also gives and must give a reasoned and careful explanation of the pros and cons before the patient gives informed consent.

In the particular case of sterilisation it is often the practice to ask for written consent of both the patient and of the spouse, although the consent of the latter may not be legally necessary.

Moral duties and legal obligations

The law of the land does not necessarily equate moral duties with legal obligations. They often go hand in hand but what may be morally right may be legally wrong. For instance it is certainly morally right for an ambulance to cross a red traffic light when going to an accident, so long as the driver is very cautious while he does it, but it is still legally wrong (see Chatterton v Olsson[3]). Sometimes doctors have conflicts between what they see as their moral duties and what they know is legally wrong. This was especially well demonstrated in the famous Bourne case[18] where a pregnancy was terminated and the doctor initially wished to claim that what he was doing was morally right correcting a moral wrong, a defence that would have failed in law; so he finally had to fall back on a second defence of medical necessity. Here not only the girl victim of a rape had given her consent to the termination of the pregnancy but her parents had begged for it and Dr Bourne had explained all the consequences of termination and of failure to terminate so far as his information at that time made clear to him.

Imparting information

How do doctors ensure that they have given adequate information to patients before obtaining their consent to investigation or treatment? There are many occasions when the doctor himself may not have the full information available to impart to the patient. For instance, certain drugs have actions or side-effects which have not been predicted from the statutory laboratory and animal tests; and some side-effects are unpredictable because these tests are not capable of assessing long-term effects. The patient may be unexpectedly idiosyncratic in his responses to certain chemicals and other treatments. So when a doctor is faced with a patient from whom, as a participant in a drug trial, informed consent is required, he is often unable to give *all* the information that should in theory be available if the patient is to make an objective decision. This failure is no one's fault.

There is also the risk of the possible interaction of drugs. If this is to be avoided the patient must inform the doctor of all the drugs that he is taking, omitting none, and this means forgetting none.

Lack of knowledge should be admitted by the doctor. It may arise in a number of ways. His knowledge may be incomplete because of elements yet to be discovered. On the other hand they may have been discovered but the doctor may not be aware of the discovery. He is therefore unable to obtain the patient's informed consent because of his own ignorance. The patient, therefore, oblivious to the fact that the information could be available, may give consent which is not fully informed and the doctor may have imparted a false idea of the value and the safety of the investigation or treatment.

From the above it follows that there are reciprocal obligations between patients and doctors – to inform as well as to treat and take treatment. Not only must the patient inform the doctor about other drugs he is taking but must also make sure, if possible, that the doctor is aware of his personal idiosyncracies, such as allergies.

The patient has even greater obligations when the doctor is acting for an insurance company. Here the law says his obligation is *uberrima fides*, which requires the most perfect frankness. Such frankness is essential when somebody to be insured for sickness or life assurance is giving a history to the examining doctor. Here, however, a problem may arise when the candidate for assurance refuses to let the doctor divulge the information given to him.

Information and consent in research trials

Dr Philip D'Arcy Hart has communicated to the authors an account of the development of consent in the early trials of streptomycin in the treatment of tuberculosis.

'I have consulted our (30-year-old) MRC reports on chemotherapy trials in tuberculosis and spoken to the statistician, Dr Ian Sutherland, responsible for many of these early isoniazid trials. I have re-read Sir Austin Bradford Hill's lecture[13] and following correspondence including protests by the Patients' Association, various papers by ourselves around these trials, contemporary (late 1940s) American reports, and contributions by Hill, Witts and Hart in a book on *Controlled Clinical Trials*.[12]

'The short answer to your questions – had we patients' consent before the streptomycin trial? – is no, in respect of Trial 1 (this was streptomycin versus no-drug).[24] The streptomycin patients were kept in a separate ward from the controls, but "were not told before admission that they were to get special treatment. Control patients did not know throughout their stay in hospital that they were control patients in a special study; they were in fact treated as they would have been in the past, the sole difference being that they had been admitted to the centre more rapidly than was normal . . . It was important for the success of the trial that the details of the control scheme should remain confidential. It is a matter of great credit to the many doctors concerned that this information was not made public throughout the 15 months of the trial . . ."

'All the ethics in the first trial were with the doctors. Was it justified to have no-drug versus streptomycin; and what about the toxicity risk? The use of no-drug control cases was clearly justified. The streptomycin supply was extremely limited and given us by the USA on the strict condition that we did such a trial, which was so far lacking. It was considered our duty not to fritter it away on uncontrolled first come, first served, but that for the benefit of mankind (the first antibiotic against tuberculosis) an accurate assessment should be made. After all, the control patients knew nothing about it and were getting the best treatment up till then available. Even though patient consent was not obtained, it is hardly conceivable that any would not have jumped at the chance of a new "cure" (there were heart-rending stories of patients who could not get the drug because we kept very closely to the scheme devised and there was no cheating).

'As to toxicity, the first paper giving vestibular damage that I can find was published (in the USA) only a month before our trial *started* so we did not know till well into the trial and from our own experience; and we assessed this complication too. Similarly with drug resistance.

'Trial 2 was streptomycin, para-amino-salicylic acid (PAS) and a combination of streptomycin and PAS.[26] "Patients were not told they were taking part in a special investigation." Again the ethics seems to have been all with the doctors, but note that *all* (and serious) cases were getting a promising drug or drugs expected to be better than nothing – drugs were still in short supply and their regimens undefined.

'Trial 3[25] was conducted similarly and no mention of consent. This trial was streptomycin/PAS versus isoniazid (first time). The circumstances were rather dramatic and seem to have justified the regimens: Squibb (USA) sent their chief medical adviser over and he presented me with a sealed envelope marked "X", which he said contained the formula of a new antituberculosis drug which needed assessing in man under MRC conditions: if we promised a controlled trial we could open the envelope, otherwise he would take it away. We accepted and it was isoniazid.

'I would guess that the ethics of patient consent only became prominent for clinical trials in the early 1960s except for one trial, namely that of "patulin" in common cold patients.[4] In this trial the volunteers were made "aware of the experimental nature of the trial". Thus in the book on *Controlled Clinical Trials* Hart[11] wrote "Patients in a trial should be informed as fully as practicable of the general objective – this does not mean knowing the particular treatment regimens – and their participation should be entirely voluntary." Professor Witts[31] wrote "The voluntary consent of the subject is regarded as essential. In an ideal world the patient would be an active intelligent participant in any clinical research of which he was the subject, but at the present time few patients have reached this level of scientific understanding. So almost at once one has to begin to qualify one's statements. Is it really necessary for a patient to agree to an experiment in which adrenocorticotrophic hormone (ACTH) and cortisone, or penicillin and aureomycin, are being compared? Of course not."'

Second opinions and changing doctors

There are many examples of patients trying to obtain a second opinion. It is a quite common experience to find that the doctor who gives the first opinion will not agree to the patient seeking a second. There may be valid medical reasons for this, but personal reasons such as loss of face by the doctor are inadequate. The patient deserves an explanation in all cases where such approval is not forthcoming, and the explanation should be a rational one.

It is customary, when a patient wishes to change his doctor, to ask the former doctor to sign the NHS medical card giving his consent to the change. The new doctor may then accept the patient at once, as he has clear evidence that his colleague has been duly informed. Some doctors will refuse consent, but this is foolhardy. It is obvious that looking after an unwilling patient must be a difficult business, to say the least.[2]

Special cases – operations

Written consent is required for almost all operations and especially for an exploratory operation. The consent form is often couched in the most vague blanket terms, such as 'I agree to whatever the surgeon deems to be necessary'. What is most likely to distress the patient is the possibility that the surgically most damaging operation may be listed on the consent form. Thus a woman may be asked to sign for surgical removal of the breast when the ultimate procedure may be only a biopsy. At the moment there is no absolute agreement among doctors that the whole breast should be removed even when a cancer of the breast is diagnosed. Increasingly, the lump and the glands that are drained by the lump are being removed while the patient retains most of her breast tissue. Yet there are some surgeons who insist that whenever a cancer is discovered the whole breast tissue must be removed. Thus the patient may be the victim of divided medical opinion although she has been informed as accurately as possible by a particular doctor and has consented accordingly. As they become more informed it is not surprising that an increasing number of women are unwilling to give their consent for mastectomy.[27] The advent of better diagnostic tests such as needle aspiration cytology and Tru-cut biopsies will, it is hoped, reduce the number of women who have to consent to mastectomy unnecessarily.[14]

On occasion the doctor also has the right not to consent to treat his patient in any way. For instance, the Abortion Act of 1967 contains a 'conscience clause' which allows a doctor who has a conscientious objection to the terms of the Act to refuse to participate in the treatment of a patient except to give 'treatment which is necessary to save the life or to prevent grave permanent injury to the physical or mental health of a pregnant woman'.[2]

Rules about operations as well as about other treatments are subject to constant revision, from place to place, from disease to disease, from decade to decade, as knowledge changes and emphases vary. This is inevitable in a fast developing science, but the rules have to be presented to the patients in such a way as to avoid destroying confidence. This requires special skills.

Patients not legally competent

So far much of what has been written concerns consent on the part of adult patients who are legally competent to give it. Those who are legally incompetent to consent are patients below a certain age, patients of any age who suffer mental illness or have impaired levels of consciousness so that they cannot adequately understand what they are being asked to consent to, and the unconscious.

In the case of children under 16 years of age the written consent of one of the parents must be obtained before a medical or surgical treatment can be undertaken, although the parent has no right to substitute his consent for that of a minor if the treatment is not in the minor's best interest.[10] This is an example of 'proxy consent' on which there appears to be no authoritative statement of legal principles in the form of statute or of case law in England and Wales.

In the case of the unconscious patient or one who is mentally ill, the consent of a parent or next of kin should be obtained. In the absence of parental consent, consent is obtained from a guardian (head master) or responsible relative. In the complete absence of consent such as in emergency treatment following road traffic accidents, treatment is normally confined to the minimum necessary to deal with the emergency.[30]

Children, particularly those in institutional homes, are potentially suitable candidates for clinical trials of new medicines for a number of reasons; for instance, they represent a stable population whose movements, diet, illnesses and so on can be easily monitored and controlled. Children have children's illnesses and it would seem logical that new treatments for children be tested on them.

In the investigation of a new drug, if there is any possible danger from its use, or if its effects on a child are unknown, no-one may authorise its use in a child. If a substance has not been used in a child before but it is known that in adults it produces desired effects similar to those produced by other substances in children, the parents alone may give permission for the trial use of the substances.[30]

It follows that comparatively few new drugs are developed for diseases of children, yet benefits to children at large depend on such research. The British Paediatric Association has issued guidelines to help Research Ethics Committees considering research involving children, and the subject is under continuous review.

The 'age of consent'

In the UK the 'age of consent' at which girls may legally have sexual intercourse remains at 16. Sexual intercourse with a girl below this age is a criminal offence. Those who facilitate this are legally aiding and abetting such a criminal offence, yet girls below 16 now frequently come to their doctors to ask for the contraceptive pill because they sleep with their boyfriends. The doctor's problem is twofold: first, should he inform the parents without the girl's permission, in order to obtain parental consent, and secondly, should he give her the pill without telling them (and ignore the legal complication) on the ground that it is better to avoid an unwanted pregnancy in an immature woman with all the ensuing problems? If parental consent is withheld, should the doctor, in the best interests of his patient, prescribe an appropriate contraceptive? He is on the horns of a dilemma which, at present, some doctors resolve by prescribing while others do not.

The fetus and consent

The case in which a pregnant woman does not consent to – and may explicitly refuse – a procedure which might affect her unborn child has most important implications. For instance, a woman refused to consent to X-ray pelvimetry during her pregnancy. Subsequently an obstetrician, who had not seen the patient before, was called in to perform the delivery. No X-ray information was available to him because of the patient's earlier decision. Attempted forceps delivery was followed by the Caesarean section birth of a brain-damaged child. Eventually the House of Lords ruled that an error of judgment made by a doctor in attempting to deliver a child by forceps was not necessarily negligent. In this unfortunate case, refusal on the part of the patient to consent to an antenatal investigation possibly contributed to the damage of a third party, namely her own child.[29]

Research

In addition to its responsibilities for curing the sick and for the prevention of illness, the medical profession is in part responsible for the advancement of knowledge on which all future cures and preventions must depend. This can be brought about only by clinical investigation on human beings. They are the only mammals in the United Kingdom for which a licence to experiment is not required. By experiment is meant anything done to someone which is not predictably of benefit to the diagnosis of his illness or its treatment.[30]

An adult may consent to research procedures provided he gives *informed consent*, which means that the patient has received all the information necessary to enable him to give consent. The need for informed consent is set out in the Declaration of Helsinki (see Appendix B), more specifically in the revised text of 1975. Consent is not binding for the duration of an experiment: the volunteer may withdraw at any time. In common law no parent or guardian has the right to give his consent to the performance of a non-therapeutic procedure in a child[17], however much this may be in the public interest: parents have no power of disposition over their child's body. But no case has yet been tested in the courts and non-therapeutic procedures occur to a significant extent. Skegg[22] and Dworkin[8] have challenged this interpretation of the law as mistaken, on the ground that medical research has no special position in law. As a child may validly consent to participate in a sport in which there is some risk of injury, so also in research procedures. Skegg concludes that children who are capable of understanding and coming to a decision are as capable as adults of giving legally effective consent to non-therapeutic experimental procedures. There is also the problem of what *is* therapeutic. For instance, for the recipient of a kidney the transplant may be life-saving but for the donor (who may be a close relative – say a brother) the operation can only be physically damaging. Is his moral reward therapeutic?

The Research Ethics Committee

There is always a great temptation to carry out an experiment for the furthering of medical knowledge without formulating a full or even partial explanation. The safeguarding of patients and healthy volunteers and the protection of doctors who take part in clinical research is therefore undertaken by research ethics committees in NHS hospitals and medical schools. These committees, consisting of both medical experts and lay persons, are meant to ensure that no unreasonable or unethical project takes place. The Report of the Royal College of Physicians[19] recommending the establishment of research ethics committees stipulated that the consent of a subject should be obtained whenever possible in the presence of a witness. It also recommended the need for particular care if a clinical investigation was proposed for children or the mentally handicapped: parents or guardians were to be consulted. The Royal College of Physicians further recommended that each research ethics committee should be small, with the sole purpose of supervising the ethics of clinical research; committees should have some medical members who were experienced clinicians and research workers, and there should be at least one lay member; committees should receive details about all proposed research investigations in their hospital or district; a full explanation should be given to the patient whenever a research investigation was not expected or intended to benefit the individual; and that particular care was needed if a clinical investigation was proposed on a subject or patient with any sort of dependent relationship with the investigator, for example, a student, laboratory technician or employee.

By definition, consent has no value if it is obtained by undue influence. But it is known that without some inducement the number of 'volunteers' for research would be seriously diminished. Beyond the compensation for loss, additional 'reward' may be financial. It may however consist of extra tuition or of the achievement of favour in the eyes of one's teacher, which is not unimportant to some medical students. Undoubtedly financial or other rewards can play a big part in the motive of a volunteer in clinical research, although another large fraction of students are moved by the altruistic desire to advance scientific knowledge. So far as the authors are able to ascertain the 'going rate' in 1982 among London students was about £15 to £20 per session, with an expectation of £45 to £60 for each project volunteered. It has been said that volunteers regard payment as contractual and so complete the study more diligently with attention to detail.[23] Perhaps ethics committees should consider the magnitude of payment when research protocols are assessed.

The motives of some volunteers are very difficult to understand, but they may be no more complicated than those of people undertaking such dangerous pursuits as pot-holing or hang-gliding. Volunteers for experiments are usually drawn from special groups such as medical students, nurses, patients, relatives of patients with particular diseases; or, more recently, from those responding to advertisements. It is important to exclude those who volunteer for reasons related to their psychopathology.

Jehovah's Witnesses

Jehovah's Witnesses present a special problem, when the risk of an operation can be manifestly increased by the refusal of the patient to accept blood transfusion. In these circumstances some surgeons refuse to give their consent to carry out operative procedures on the patients, a decision that may be more emotional than based on a total assessment of the best needs of patients. The problem is almost insoluble when an operation is for haemorrhage and the Jehovah's Witness is a fully conscious adult suffering from blood loss. When the Jehovah's Witness is a child or is mentally ill he can be made a ward of court and permission for blood transfusion can be granted by a magistrate. If the transfusion is given on a magistrate's order there is a danger that the parents might reject the child.

It was thought that when an operation that could be planned for months ahead was to be carried out on a Jehovah's Witness, the patient could be bled one or two units of blood and the blood stored for use during the operation. The advantage of this procedure was that the loss of a unit of blood (about a pint) would be made good within two to three weeks by the manufacture of fresh red blood cells. If blood was lost during the operation, it could be replaced from the patient's own stored blood without the need to use somebody else's blood as a transfusion. Recently, however, Jehovah's Witnesses have claimed that even this is forbidden by their religion, which forbids blood to be 'taken' in any form.[28]

It has been stated that some surgeons in a life threatening emergency may decide to use blood products without consent.[6] Other surgeons, however, fearing litigation, prefer to hand the patient over to colleagues, or else simply refuse to operate.

In fact in most operations really careful surgeons, by dint of operating very slowly and meticulously, can avoid the need for blood transfusion, although the operation can be much more hazardous if there is no blood available for the patient should an emergency develop. This does not apply to open heart surgery where blood transfusion is essential and where in any case the patient's own blood has to circulate round a machine in which it is oxygenated, separate from but connected by piping with the patient, while the patient's own heart is artificially inhibited from beating during the operation.

Industrial medicine

It is customary now for big industrial concerns and other businesses to appoint doctors with special qualifications in industrial medicine. One purpose of such appointments is to avoid the employees wasting time in their own general practitioners' waiting rooms (which may lose them a half day's work) instead of a few minutes lost picking up a prescription in the factory; another is that the doctors give a service which, by the special skills and knowledge they have acquired, is the most suitable for patients employed in a particular industry. The doctor then has a dual loyalty: to his employers who pay his salary, and to the patients. The patients then have two doctors to consult, the family doctor whenever they wish and whenever they are away from work, and the works doctor together with his nurses and other assistants whenever needed at work, either for an emergency or in order to save time.

The interests of the employer and the patient seldom clash. They are usually identical, namely for the employee to be as fit as possible for the job in hand. Difficulty may arise, however, where the doctor comes to realise that somebody looking after a potentially dangerous machine is quite unsuited for the job by reason of illness, as for instance epilepsy.

The doctor usually manages to persuade the patient to stop doing the work or to change to another job; but if he is unable to do so, there is a conflict of interests that is more apparent than real. Obviously, if someone is dangerous working a machine or driving a lorry he is a danger to others as well as a danger to himself. If he refuses permission for his illness to be revealed there is an ethical problem to be resolved. Each case has to be decided by the doctor on its own merits. In these circumstances he can turn to his defence society for advice, which it will always give; or it will support him if he has taken a step that leads to his being sued.

Insurance examinations

In examinations for life assurance or for sickness assurance a conflict does not arise because the contract is between the doctor and the assurance company. The sick person seeking insurance can either agree to his family doctor letting the assurance company know all he has been told, or withdraw his application for insurance. If he seeks to conceal vital information then his insurance is not valid (p 95 *supra*).

The state and the doctor

The state has become one of the biggest employers of labour in the country. The Department of Health and Social Security alone employs nearly a million people and so doctors working for the state are often in a position similar to that of doctors working for industrial firms.

Without question, doctors employed in the National Health Service are, so far as consent is concerned, in exactly the same position as doctors in private practice, except that they derive their income indirectly from their National Health Service patients, whereas in private practice income is derived directly from the patient; but this fact should not alter the relationship with patients.

Doctors in the armed forces sometimes encounter a difficult conflict of interests brought about by their special duty to keep their patients in fighting condition. Fighting, on the other hand, may lead to the ill-health of the patient. The doctor's loyalty to his service should not normally conflict with his loyalty to his patient because the interest of both is to keep as many healthy people in good health as possible. Yet, in order to see the service achieve the numbers needed for a particular combat operation, he may be tempted to certify as fit someone who may not be totally well, with or without that person's consent.

Prisoners

A special area for consideration is the quality of the consent given by prisoners. It is not unknown for doctors to be called to 'quieten' prisoners with sedatives. Although prisoners may agree to receive such drugs, this consent is sometimes obtained by rather questionable methods of persuasion short of force. The mental state of a prisoner may be more conducive to his acceptance of a treatment than that of a free person, but the opposite is usually the case. Giving an injection to a patient without his consent constitutes an assault, whether the patient is a prisoner or free. The problem is especially applicable in the case of a pregnant prisoner where not only her interests but those of her fetus have to be considered, as well as the interests of the other inmates of the prison. The injection that calms may help all three, but what if the patient refuses it?

It is very tempting to invite prisoners to participate in medical research. The advantages are clear: the prisoner will turn up day after day for observation; the observations will usually be accurate because the external conditions will not change and, except for quarrels with other prisoners or with the officers, there will be few, if any, external factors altering the physical state of the prisoner on whom the research is being carried out. The advantages, however, are much more limited than would at first appear. Prisoners cannot be used unless they volunteer or respond to the most gentle persuasion. Those who volunteer tend to want to please, just as some students do. Wanting to please in experiments where the impressions or subjective feelings of the person treated enter into the results claimed (such as feeling calmer after being given a sedative) invalidates the result entirely. There are dangers even where the subjective feelings of the patients are not involved. For instance, people living in closed communities react differently from those out in the open. In one classic but unpublished experiment to test a new drug for a sexually transmitted disease, doctors were unaware that the disease usually quietened down after a few weeks without sexual intercourse and that therefore the symptoms abated, even though some of the bacteria still lurked in the body; when, moreover, the patients developed jaundice due to the drug, the doctors were also fooled into believing that the jaundice was an infective type of hepatitis. A clinical trial performed outside the prison produced totally different results and the prison trial was shown to be valueless. So, ethically experiments on prisoners may be debatable, and practically they may be without value.

The mentally ill

The treatment of mentally ill patients is in process of change. This process has gone on for the last few decades and is still continuing. The Council for Science and Society has recently argued that there is a need for a new approach on the issue of consent.[5] This paper recommends that a non-medical 'patient's advocate' should also give consent. This 'patient's advocate' could be a relative, friend or one of a panel of lay members and lawyers. Obviously such a change would work only if the patient's friend was a responsible person who could, while not rubber-stamping the doctor's decisions, at least understand the doctor's aims.

Decisions on the part of the patient are not made easier by confused public debate about controversial medical issues. The patients are thereby subjected to considerable anxiety which makes their ability to consent more difficult.

Doctors in mental hospitals often give psychotropic drugs. Many of the patients are unwilling residents in the hospitals. A patient admitted involuntarily to a mental hospital on the recommendation of two doctors (only one of whom has to be specially experienced in mental disorders) under the provisions of part IV of the Mental Health Act 1959 can be treated in any way the psychiatrist thinks correct, and this may include injections with drugs or physical restraint, although the latter is used less often nowadays. The rationale behind such treatment is that it is in the patient's own interests. While it is true that the patient's interests are often paramount they tend to coincide with the interests of others. In his very full discussion paper Gostin argues that the forcibly detained psychiatric patient may still be competent to give or to refuse consent.[10]

Is the doctor-patient relationship contractual?

We now come to the task of attempting to define or categorise the nature of the relationship between the doctor and his patient. The title given to that relationship seems to vary according to the financial relationship between them. If money passes from patient to doctor in return for the doctor's services a legal contract has been made. However, the definition is not so clear as far as contract is concerned if no money passes, or if the doctor's financial reward is paid indirectly by the agency of the state, as it is when the doctor works for the National Health Service.

What is the moral relationship between the two, and what is the psychological relationship? It should at all times be one of mutual trust; but is it always? Clearly it is not. Bernard Shaw attempted to define the relationship in his preface written in 1911 to his 1906 play *The Doctor's Dilemma*, but he did it rather superficially, for him, and even with postscripts added in 1930 and 1933[20,21], his explanation of the relationship between doctor and patient, doctors and science and doctors and the government is unclear, perhaps because his mind was so clouded by his own prejudices and propensities. But then many patients have a bias in one direction or another, and many doctors have too.

The observer's view of the relationship may well depend heavily on his own profession and degree of learning; it will differ according to whether he is a philosopher, a lawyer, a doctor who is a patient himself, a research scientist or the man on the Clapham omnibus.

Relationship must vary also between individual doctors and their individual patients; it must depend somewhat on the length and type of treatment being given and received. A psychiatrist's relationship with his patient must be totally different to that of a surgeon with his. Yet he will attempt in the broadest way to discuss the moral and the legal relationship. The psychological relationship is too diffuse to be discussed in this paper.

The moral and legal relationship – mutual trust

Modern writers' sentiments about doctors have been expressed by Ashley and O'Rourke[1], who state: 'The medical profession, like any true profession, must rest not on bargaining but on trust, and it provides a service that is concerned with life and death, matters so precious as to be priceless . . . Nor is there any price of the service of a physician in the battle to live.' These authors say that the remuneration given to doctors is not so much payment for a specific service as a stipend given to support them so that they can serve those in need. Hence in private medicine it is frequently the case that the poor are served almost free, or quite freely, whereas the well off are charged what they can afford.

The relationship between a solicitor and his client is certainly a contractual one, as is the relationship between a hospital doctor and his employing authority. In this case it is a contract in writing and usually under seal. But the relationship between a doctor employed by a district health authority and a patient may not be completely contractual. Is it quasi-contractual? Or is it, as Dunstan suggests, more truly a covenant?[7] On the doctor-patient relationship he stated '. . . and the physician was and is like the priest in this, that he has to offer continuing care for his patient, whether he can remedy his ills, in the sense of curing him, or not. He has to serve his interest, in remedy or recovery if he can, in his living with the least distress while he lives, and in dying when in time he comes to die. This is the object of the doctor-patient relationship.'

The language of contract is sometimes used for this relationship. Here care must be exercised in generalisation, because of the different systems in which doctors work – some in government service like the armed forces, some in a national health service or Medicare scheme, some in partnerships, some alone in private practice. But we may enquire what is the nature of a contract? It is an undertaking to perform a stated service in consideration of a stated return, the one related to and limited by the other. Dunstan points out that the language of contract can be used of the economic relation between a doctor and his employing hospital or government authority, but he questions whether contractual terms can be used without distortion to describe the relationship between the doctor and the patient.

The Medical Defence Union (in a letter to Elliot E Philipp) has very kindly given the following view:

> 'There is no general answer to whether or not a contract exists between the patient and the doctor. It depends on what the doctor is. For example, in NHS hospitals there is certainly not, in legal terms, any contract between doctor and patient. In private practice there most certainly is a contract between doctor and patient. With regard to the NHS GP, there may or may not exist a contract. There are opposing schools of thought. Our principal solicitor thinks there is in the sense that the patient will have

signed an NHS form applying to be put on the list of a particular doctor and that the doctor will be remunerated for any services which he renders to that patient via the capitation fee system which exists in the general medical services. The answer, therefore, is that as so often "it all depends on the facts of the particular case". . . . Also, we do not think the word "covenant" would be at all appropriate in the context of relations between doctor and patient.'

In our discussions Fr Brendan Soane informs us that he considers that a patient consults a doctor without making any contract with him. The doctor is, or should be, the person who puts his expertise at the service of suffering humanity. If this is so, the language of contract does not seem to do justice to the precise nature of the relationship between doctor and patient.

Our colleague Peter Byrne has pointed out that Dunstan directed his comments to what the relationship ought to be, whereas the Medical Defence Union has tried to express what it may be in law; but here there is clear evidence that observers will view the relationship differently even when they have given much thought to the problem.

It may well be also that, as we have pointed out earlier in this paper, the reasoning the doctor gives to the patient when he tries to explain what he is going to do in advance may be scanty and ill-formed. This is precisely what Bernard Shaw said in his preface. He pointed out that doctors are not as scientific as they think they are and because they are practical in their dealings with patients their deep scientific knowledge may be different from that of pure scientists. Furthermore, events and developments may, occasionally, make a nonsense of the plans set forth by the doctor, although usually this will not be so.

As a result it is not realistic to demand that medical treatment should be subjected at every detailed stage to prior consent on behalf of the patients. To demand this may be to turn the doctor-patient relationship into one that is unambiguously contractual. The limitations this would impose could be unworkable and adverse to patients' interests; doctors should resist a demand so to tie their practice to consent as to leave them without freedom to act upon their judgment of what is best for their patients. Put another way: morally-speaking the relationship ought to involve trust on the part of the patient and fidelity on the part of the doctor. But both of these things imply conduct that is not at every point governed or governable by prior agreement. Where there is trust, more may be given in necessity than has been agreed upon or even foreseen.

References

1 Ashley, B M and O'Rourke, K D. *Health care ethics: a theological analysis*. St Louis, Catholic Health Association, 1978. p 113.

2 Barlow, D T C. *British general practice: a personal guide for students*. London, H K Lewis, 1973. pp 68, 81–84.

3 *Chatterton v Olsson and another*. 1 All ER 257 QBD. (*The Times*, 7 February, 1981.)

4 Clinical trial of patulin in the common cold: report of the Patulin Clinical Trials Committee. Medical Research Council. *Lancet*, vol 2, no 6316. 16 September, 1944. pp 373–375.

5 Council for Science and Society. *Treating the troublesome: report of a working party*. (Chairman, John Ziman.) London, Council for Science and Society, 1981.

6 Drew, N C. The pregnant Jehovah's Witness. *Journal of Medical Ethics*, vol 7, no 3. September, 1981. pp 137–139.

7 Dunstan, G R. The doctor-patient relationship. In: Wood, C. ed. *Health and the family*. London, Academic Press; New York, Grune and Stratton, 1979. pp 185–192.

8 Dworkin, Gerald. Legality of consent to non therapeutic medical research on infants and young children. *Archives of Disease in Childhood*, vol 53, no 6. June, 1978. pp 443–446.

9 Eysenck, H and Eysenck, M. *Mindwatching*. London, Book Club Associates, 1981. pp 139–145.

10 Gostin, Larry O. Observations on consent to treatment and review of clinical judgement in psychiatry: a discussion paper. *Journal of the Royal Society of Medicine*, vol 74, no 10. October, 1981. pp 742–752.

11 Hart, P D. The organization of controlled clinical trials. In: Hill, A B. ed. *Controlled clinical trials: papers delivered at the conference convened by the Council for International Organizations of Medical Sciences*. Oxford, Blackwell Scientific, 1960. pp 145–150.
12 Hill, A B. Aims and ethics. In: Hill, A B. ed. *Controlled clinical trials: papers delivered at the conference convened by the Council for International Organizations of Medical Sciences*. Oxford, Blackwell Scientific, 1960. pp 3–7.
13 Hill, Sir Austin Bradford. Medical ethics and controlled trials. *British Medical Journal*, vol I, no 5337. 20 April, 1963. pp 1043–1049.
14 Nixon, S J and Forrest, A P M. Consent to mastectomy [letter]. *British Medical Journal*, vol 281, no 6253. 29 November, 1980. pp 1492–1493.
15 Norell, J S. Introduction. In: Balint, Enid and Norell, J S. eds. *Six minutes for the patient: interactions in general practice consultation*. London, Tavistock, 1973. pp ix–xxi.
16 O'Hanrahan, M and O'Malley, K. Compliance with drug treatment. *British Medical Journal*, vol 283, no 6286. 25 July, 1981. pp 298–300.
17 Responsibility in investigations on human subjects: statement by Medical Research Council. *British Medical Journal*, vol II, no 5402. 18 July, 1964. pp 178–180.
18 *Rex v Bourne*, Central Criminal Court. 3 All ER. 615; (1939) 1 KB. 687.
19 Royal College of Physicians. *Report of the committee on the supervision of the ethics of clinical research investigations in institutions*. London, Royal College of Physicians, 1973.
20 Shaw, G B. The doctor's dilemma. In: *Complete plays*. London, Constable, 1931. pp 503, 545.
21 Shaw, G B. *Prefaces*. London, Odhams Press, 1938. pp 237–280.
22 Skegg, P D G. English law relating to experimentation on children. *Lancet*, vol II, no 8041. 8 October, 1977. pp 754–755.
23 Smith, Robert N. Safeguards for healthy volunteers in drug studies. *Lancet*, vol II, no 7932. 6 September, 1975. pp 449–450.
24 Streptomycin treatment of pulmonary tuberculosis: A Medical Research Council investigation. *British Medical Journal*, vol II, no 4582. 30 October, 1948. pp 769–782.

25 The treatment of pulmonary tuberculosis with isoniazid: an interim report to the Medical Research Council by their Chemotherapy Trials Committee. *British Medical Journal*, vol 2, no 4787. 4 October, 1952. pp 735–746.

26 Treatment of pulmonary tuberculosis with streptomycin and para-amino-salicylic acid: a Medical Research Council investigation. *British Medical Journal*, vol 2, no 4688. 11 November, 1950. pp 1073–1085.

27 Thomson, H J and others. Consent for mastectomy. *British Medical Journal*, vol 281, no 6248. 25 October, 1980. pp 1097–1098.

28 Watch Tower Bible and Tract Society of Pennsylvania. *Jehovah's Witnesses and the question of blood.* New York, International Bible Students Association, 1977.

29 *Whitehouse v Jordan*. 1 WLR. 246; 1 All ER. 267. 1981.

30 Wilkinson, A W. Consent. In: Duncan, A S and others. eds. *Dictionary of medical ethics*. Revised edition. London, Darton, Longman and Todd, 1981. pp 113–117.

31 Witts, L J. The ethics of controlled clinical trials. In: Hill, A B. ed. *Controlled clinical trials: papers delivered at the conference convened by the Council for International Organizations of Medical Sciences*. Oxford, Blackwell Scientific, 1960. pp 8–13.

The authors are grateful to Dr Philip D'Arcy Hart CBE MD FRCP for the information given on pp 95–97.

Appendix A

THE NUREMBERG CODE[1]

On 19 August 1947, a War Crimes tribunal at Nürnberg rendered judgment on 23 German defendants, mostly physicians, who were accused of crimes involving experiments on human subjects. The judgment laid down ten standards to which physicians must conform when carrying out experiments on human subjects, as follows:

Permissible medical experiments

The great weight of the evidence before us is to the effect that certain types of medical experiments on human beings, when kept within reasonably well-defined bounds, conform to the ethics of the medical profession generally. The protagonists of the practice of human experimentation justify their views on the basis that such experiments yield results for the good of society that are unprocurable by other methods or means of study. All agree, however, that certain basic principles must be observed in order to satisfy moral, ethical and legal concepts:

1 The voluntary consent of the human subject is absolutely essential. This means that the person involved should have legal capacity to give consent; should be so situated as to be able to exercise free power of choice, without the intervention of any element of force, fraud, deceit, duress, overreaching, or other ulterior form of constraint or coercion; and should have sufficient knowledge and comprehension of the elements of the subject matter involved as to enable him to make an understanding and enlightened decision. This latter element requires that before the acceptance of an affirmative decision by the experimental subject there should be made known to him the nature, duration, and purpose of the experiment; the method and means by which it is to be conducted; all inconveniences and hazards

reasonably to be expected; and the effects upon his health or person which may possibly come from his participation in the experiment.

The duty and responsibility for ascertaining the quality of the consent rests upon each individual who initiates, directs, or engages in the experiment. It is a personal duty and responsibility which may not be delegated to another with impunity.

2 The experiment should be such as to yield fruitful results for the good of society, unprocurable by other methods or means of study, and not random and unnecessary in nature.

3 The experiment should be so designed and based on the results of animal experimentation and a knowledge of the natural history of the disease or other problem under study that the anticipated results justify the performance of the experiment.

4 The experiment should be so conducted as to avoid all unnecessary physical and mental suffering and injury.

5 No experiment should be conducted where there is an *a priori* reason to believe that death or disabling injury will occur; except, perhaps, in those experiments where the experimental physicians also serve as the subjects.

6 The degree of risk to be taken should never exceed that determined by the humanitarian importance of the problem to be solved by the experiment.

7 Proper preparations should be made, and adequate facilities provided to protect the experimental subject against even remote possibilities of injury, disability, or death.

8 The experiment should be conducted only by scientifically qualified persons. The highest degree of skill and care should be required through all stages of the experiment of those who conduct or engage in the experiment.

9 During the course of the experiment the human subject should be at liberty to bring the experiment to an end if he has reached the physical or mental state where continuation of the experiment seems to him to be impossible.

10 During the course of the experiment the scientist in charge must be prepared to terminate the experiment at any stage, if he has probable cause to believe, in the exercise of

the good faith, superior skill, and careful judgment required of him, that a continuation of the experiment is likely to result in injury, disability, or death to the experimental subject.

References

1 Wolstenholme, G E W and O'Connor, Maeve. eds. Appendix 1: the Nuremberg code. In: Ciba Foundation. *Ethics in medical progress: with special reference to transplantation.* London, J and A Churchill, 1966.

Appendix B

THE DECLARATION OF HELSINKI[1]

The World Medical Association, in 1964, drew up a Code of Ethics on Human Experimentation. This Code was known as the Declaration of Helsinki, after the city where the meeting which gave rise to it took place. It was subsequently revised, in 1975, at the meeting of the World Medical Association which took place in Tokyo in that year, as follows:

The Declaration of Helsinki

Recommendations guiding medical doctors in biomedical research involving human subjects

Introduction

It is the mission of the medical doctor to safeguard the health of the people. His or her knowledge and conscience are dedicated to the fulfilment of this mission.

The Declaration of Geneva of the World Medical Association binds the doctor with the words: 'The health of my patient will be my first consideration,' and the International Code of Medical Ethics declares that, 'Any act or advice which could weaken physical or mental resistance of a human being may be used only in his interest'.

The purpose of biomedical research involving human subjects must be to improve diagnostic, therapeutic and prophylactic procedures and the understanding of the aetiology and pathogenesis of disease.

In current medical practice most diagnostic, therapeutic or prophylactic procedures involve hazards. This applies *a fortiori* to biomedical research.

Medical progress is based on research which ultimately must rest in part on experimentation involving human subjects. In the field of biomedical research a fundamental distinction must be recognised between medical research in which the aim is essentially diagnostic or therapeutic for a patient, and medical research the essential object of which is purely scientific and without direct diagnostic or therapeutic value to the person subjected to the research.

Special caution must be exercised in the conduct of research which may affect the environment, and the welfare of animals used for research must be respected.

Because it is essential that the results of laboratory experiments be applied to human beings to further scientific knowledge and to help suffering humanity, the World Medical Association has prepared the following recommendations as a guide to every doctor in biomedical research involving human subjects. They should be kept under review in the future. It must be stressed that the standards as drafted are only a guide to physicians all over the world. Doctors are not relieved from criminal, civil and ethical responsibilities under the laws of their own countries.

I *Basic principles*

1 Biomedical research involving human subjects must conform to generally accepted scientific principles and should be based on adequately performed laboratory and animal experimentation and on a thorough knowledge of the scientific tradition.

2 The design and performance of each experimental procedure involving human subjects should be clearly formulated in an experimental protocol which should be transmitted to a specially appointed independent committee for consideration, comment and guidance.

3 Biomedical research involving human subjects should be conducted only by scientifically qualified persons and under the supervision of a clinically competent medical person. The responsibility for the human subject must always rest with a medically qualified person and never rest on the subject of the research, even though the subject has given his or her consent.

4 Biomedical research involving human subjects cannot legitimately be carried out unless the importance of the objective is in proportion to the inherent risk to the subject.

5 Every biomedical research project involving human subjects should be preceded by careful assessment of predictable risks in comparison with forseeable benefits to the subject or to others. Concern for the interests of the subject must always prevail over the interest of science and society.

6 The right of the research subject to safeguard his or her integrity must always be respected. Every precaution should be taken to respect the privacy of the subject and to minimise the impact of the study on the subject's physical and mental integrity and on the personality of the subject.

7 Doctors should abstain from engaging in research projects involving human subjects unless they are satisfied that the hazards involved are believed to be predictable. Doctors should cease any investigation if the hazards are found to outweigh the potential benefits.

8 In publication of the results of his or her research, the doctor is obliged to preserve the accuracy of the results. Reports of experimentation not in accordance with the principles laid down in this Declaration should not be accepted for publication.

9 In any research on human beings, each potential subject must be adequately informed of the aims, methods, anticipated benefits and potential hazards of the study and the discomfort it may entail. He or she should be informed that he or she is at liberty to abstain from participation in the study and that he or she is free to withdraw his or her consent to participation at any time. The doctor should then obtain the subject's freely-given informed consent, preferably in writing.

10 When obtaining informed consent for the research project the doctor should be particularly cautious if the subject is in a dependent relationship to him or her or may consent under duress. In that case the informed consent should be obtained by a doctor who is not engaged in the investigation and who is completely independent of this official relationship.

11 In case of legal incompetence, informed consent should be obtained from the legal guardian in accordance with national legislation. Where physical or mental incapacity

makes it impossible to obtain informed consent, or when the subject is a minor, permission from the responsible relative replaces that of the subject in accordance with national legislation.

12 The research protocol should always contain a statement of the ethical considerations involved and should indicate that the principles enunciated in the present Declaration are complied with.

II *Medical research combined with professional care (clinical research)*

1 In the treatment of the sick person, the doctor must be free to use a new diagnostic and therapeutic measure, if in his or her judgment it offers hope of saving life, re-establishing health or alleviating suffering.

2 The potential benefits, hazards and discomfort of a new method should be weighed against the advantages of the best current diagnostic and therapeutic methods.

3 In any medical study, every patient – including those of a control group, if any – should be assured of the best proven diagnostic and therapeutic method.

4 The refusal of the patient to participate in a study must never interfere with the doctor-patient relationship.

5 If the doctor considers it essential not to obtain informed consent, the specific reasons for this proposal should be stated in the experimental protocol for transmission to the independent committee.

6 The doctor can combine medical research with professional care, the objective being the acquisition of new medical knowledge, only to the extent that medical research is justified by its potential diagnostic or therapeutic value for the patient.

III *Non-therapeutic biomedical research involving human subjects (non-clinical biomedical research)*

1 In the purely scientific application of medical research carried out on a human being, it is the duty of the doctor to remain the protector of the life and health of that person on whom biomedical research is being carried out.

2 The subjects should be volunteers – either healthy persons or patients – for whom the experimental design is not related to the patient's illness.
3 The investigator or the investigating team should discontinue the research if in his/her or their judgment it may, if continued, be harmful to the individual.
4 In research on man, the interests of science and society should never take precedence over considerations related to the well-being of the subject.

References

Duncan, A S and others. eds. *Dictionary of medical ethics*. Revised edition. London, Darton, Longman and Todd, New York, Crossroad, 1981. pp 132–135.

INDEX